WITH A SIEGE BATTERY IN FRANCE.

303 SIEGE BATTERY, R.G.A.

1916—1919.

1919.

PREFACE.

This history makes no claim to any literary merit, and is only a simple record of our doings in England, Belgium, France, and Germany. It has been hurriedly compiled from insufficient data, helped out by recollections of many members of the Battery.

Our thanks are due principally to Bombardier Trotter and his assistants, Bombardier Birrell, and Gunner Beardsworth, to Mr. C. H. Ledward for the chapter on " O.P's," to Signaller Collyer, who typed the manuscript on a "dud" German typewriter, and to Major C. R. Molyneux, M.C., for kind permission to print the poem on page 74, which, we understand, was actually inspired by our No. 1 gun.

If the story which it tells serves in the future to enliven any reunion of former members of "303" by helping out their memories of "The Great Adventure," or to make clear to any of our friends in after years the nature of our doings, the labours of the contributors will be well repaid.

Bonn, 1919.   J. O. K. DELAP.

CONTENTS.

ILLUSTRATIONS.

WITH A SIEGE BATTERY
IN FRANCE.

CHAPTER I.

EMPLOYMENT OF HEAVY ARTILLERY.

In the first days of the war the use of heavy artillery was not understood to any extent; so little, in fact, that until some weeks after the war had begun, full use was not made of the heavy artillery which we possessed on the outbreak of hostilities. The important part which heavy artillery was to play was soon apparent, and an ambitious programme of gun construction was begun and continued for several years, until a very large number of heavy batteries were in the field.

Mobile heavy artillery was intended to be used against forts containing guns in position, and its use for this purpose was so deadly that the fort, as such, became obsolete within a fortnight. The French defensive system of ring fortresses, such as at Liege and Namur, was shown to be incorrect. As soon as the German heavy artillery reached Liege a bombardment was opened on the cupola forts there, and these were blown to pieces. Namur fell almost without a fight.

Fixed forts being shown to be easily vulnerable, it became evident that the best defence for guns for land use lay in concealment, and armoured and concreted positions were almost entirely given up. This introduced the principle of camouflage for battery positions, and the importance of this has increased continuously with the improvement in observing and "spotting" appliances.

During the first year of the war heavy artillery as a general rule confined its operations to shooting at infantry strong points, trenches, wire entanglements, roads, buildings, and places in the enemy's forward areas. It was only in the later years that heavy artillery took to shooting at the enemy's heavy artillery. The description of "artillery duels" in the early days really meant that the enemy's heavy artillery shot at our infantry, and our artillery shot at the enemy's infantry—a bloodless battle for us, but unpleasant for the infantry. The tendency has been, ever since those days, for heavy artillery to come nearer and nearer to the line in trench warfare, and to engage targets further and further behind the enemy lines, so much so that of late years our targets have been almost exclusively enemy batteries and back areas, while the enemy infantry has been attended to, from the artillery point of view, by our field artillery and trench mortars. With this increase in what is known as "counter-battery" work the problem of concealment already referred to became more important.

The various methods in use for "spotting" enemy batteries included (first) ground observation from observation posts situated on high ground or in a commanding position of some kind, e.g., up a tree, or on the top of a house; (second) balloon observation from a line of captive balloons flying behind the heavy artillery area ; (third) aeroplane observation, either from behind the infantry lines, or from over the enemy lines and artillery areas. Another method in use for detecting the presence and position of hostile batteries was known as "sound ranging," whereby the actual position of a gun could be decided by noting the exact time at which the sound of the discharge of the gun reached certain points behind our lines.

The means used to counter this constant watchfulness by both sides were these : for concealment against ground observers, batteries were invariably sited behind cover, so that the gun position could not be seen from any point in the enemy lines ; concealment from balloons has always been very difficult, and these were sometimes regarded as the gunners' worst enemy ; to safeguard ourselves against aeroplane observers, special sentries were trained to stand behind the battery and give warning of the approach of a hostile aeroplane, when fire would immediately cease, the guns be covered up, and everything possible done to conceal the battery. Means were devised for confusing the enemy's sound-rangers, but they should not be dealt with here. Thus a constant competition took place between the arts of concealment and observation. A battery once "spotted," so that its location was exactly known, was thenceforward of very much less value than a battery whose position remained unknown to the enemy.

When a battery which had been "spotted" opened fire on any point behind the enemy's lines that he wished to protect, neutralising fire would immediately be brought to bear on that battery by the enemy, and if the location of the battery was exactly known, this was likely to render it impossible for the battery to continue firing without incurring casualties. If, on the other hand, the "spotted" battery had to take part in an operation in support of our infantry, either in attack or defence, and was shelled while doing so, the probability of damage and casualties became very much greater, because in those circumstances a battery could not cease fire though heavily engaged.

The actual employment of heavy artillery in this war may roughly be divided into two groups. Brigades are detailed for (a) counter-battery work, in which case they shoot principally at enemy batteries ; (b) bombardment, for shooting at roads, trenches, strong points, etc. The natural tendency is for the counter-battery brigades to be placed nearer the enemy line than the bombardment brigades, in order that their fire shall reach the enemy battery areas.

The conditions under which heavy artillery has been used are (first) stationary or trench warfare ; (second) in attack ; and (third) for a short period, in defence. Since the autumn of 1917 a change has taken place in the employment of heavy artillery in attack. The old method in preparation for an attack was to mass a large body of heavy artillery behind our lines and to arrange for each battery, as soon as it was in position, to register its "line" and engage targets in the usual way ; then, when the day arrived on which the attack was timed to take place, all these batteries would open fire on the targets allotted to them—some on enemy batteries, some on roads, trenches, strong points, etc.

The result of this increase in the volume of fire in some particular sector of our front was that the enemy also massed heavy artillery behind his line in an endeavour to meet our fire, and the sector in which the attack was planned was "given away" to the enemy. It had also this disadvantage, that for several days, possibly even weeks, before the infantry attack opened, an artillery duel of constantly increasing intensity took place between our batteries and the enemy's, with the result that on the day of attack, not only were the locations of most of our batteries "spotted," but that the enemy had timely warning of our intention to attack him,.and was able to take defensive measures.

On the day selected for the attack the heavy artillery would open with a preliminary bombardment on the enemy defences lasting some hours. This was designed to cut his wire entanglements and demoralise his infantry, but it also gave him time to bring up his reserves before our infantry attack took place.

The modern method has been, first, to decide where an attack should be made, and then, with the utmost secrecy, to put a great mass of batteries in position, doing all movement of guns and ammunition by night, and carefully concealing all traces of new work by day. All the new batteries would remain silent until the hour fixed for the commencement of the attack. When the moment arrived the heavy artillery opened fire on its allotted tasks, which, in a modern battle, are all targets at some distance behind the enemy's front line. The field artillery laid a concentrated barrage along the enemy's front line, but lifted from this in about four minutes. During this time our infantry were getting out of their trenches and crossing "no man's land," so that the enemy was attacked before he had time to recover from the initial shock of the bombardment.

The field artillery barrage, which started on the front line and lifted after four minutes, continued, as a rule, in "bounds" of a hundred yards at a time, up to the limit of its range, and was usually assisted by the bombardment brigades of heavy artillery. The attacking infantry thus advanced for several hours close behind the moving barrage.

The old method, then, consisted of long, powerful artillery preparation, while the new method was entirely dependent upon surprise.

The Battle of Cambrai, in 1917, was the first occasion on which the surprise attack was tried, and its success, as a surprise, was complete. All the British attacks since that date, which were undertaken with the object of breaking through defensive positions, were done on this plan. The advantage to the heavy artillery of this type of attack was very great. In the old days we had several weeks of heavy firing, with the enemy in increasing artillery strength trying to stop us, whereas nowadays we open fire in an attack with every confidence that the enemy does not know where we are, and therefore cannot reply effectively. As already explained, any batteries which have been in action in their position, and have been "spotted" by the enemy, are at a great disadvantage as compared with the batteries brought in for the attack.

One of the features of the modern battles has been the rapid advance of the batteries forming the mobile brigades. In some cases a " flying section" of each of these batteries has been ordered to pull out and move forward at the very beginning of the engagement, and has been out and pulling across the enemy front line while the infantry were attacking the enemy support line.

Counter-battery work has been an important feature of all the surprise attacks. In addition to laying as heavy a barrage as possible on the enemy defences it is important to prevent his batteries interfering with our infantry. In preparation for this the corps counter-battery offices compile lists of the exact locations of as many enemy batteries as possible, so that on the day all these may be subjected to neutralising fire. In some cases each battery of the counter-battery brigades would be given as its target one enemy battery, but in some of the battles an improvement on this system was introduced, in which each battery of six guns fired at six different enemy batteries. Conversely, each enemy battery received the fire from one gun of six British batteries, which lessened its chances of escaping damage. The success of this method was very marked in the Battle of Amiens on 8th August, 1918, where an inspection of the enemy batteries on the morning of the attack showed that almost every one of them had been successfully engaged. Many guns were seen surrounded by dead detachments, with the layer at the sight, the " No. 2" with the lanyard in his hand, and ammunition numbers bringing up the shell— all killed at their posts.

During the autumn and winter of 1917 it was a common practice to place the 6″ Howitzer batteries of the counter-battery brigades very close up to the front line, in order to give them the range necessary for their particular work. This battery, after the Battle of Cambrai, remained for three months within 1,100 yards of the line, being 1,000 yards in front of the field artillery positions, and under not infrequent bursts of machine gun fire.

During the period following the great enemy attacks of the spring of 1918, batteries were sited further back to enable them to keep up defensive fire for a longer period and to obviate their capture in the event of an enemy break-through, and during this time alternative positions were prepared to cover the trench systems constructed as rear lines of defence.

Experience has been gained in the successful advances of the autumn of 1918, while the retreats of the spring of that year gave us the bitter experience of being driven back. We have occupied as many as four different positions in one day of an advance, and have taken up three different positions in one day of a retirement.

It may be mentioned without undue boasting that neither in the retirement after the Battle of Cambrai nor in the long retreat from in in front of Bapaume to Mailly-Maillet on the Ancre did we leave behind any guns, essential stores, or a single round of ammunition. This was largely due to the work done by the section of the A.S.C. motor transport attached to the battery.

To understand the working of a mobile brigade of heavy artillery in the field, one must realise that lighter types of heavy artillery are either horse or tractor drawn. Mobile brigades consist of 60-pounder and 6″ Howitzer batteries, the 60-pounders being horse drawn, the Howitzers tractor drawn.

This battery, throughout most of its service in France and Belgium, has had six guns, each drawn on the road by a mechanical tractor, having all four wheels driven (known as an F.W.D.). There are, in addition, 15 lorries, each capable of carrying 3 tons, allotted as follows:—

9 for ammunition,
4 for stores and gun parts,
1 for rations,
1 for moving the stores belonging to the A.S.C. section attached to the battery.

All the movements described in the history of the battery were carried out with the above mechanical transport, excepting in the one case of the Battle of Cambrai, November, 1917, when the battery was horsed for the occasion by a heavy battery's horses to render it more mobile on ground softened by the rains of autumn. This was considered necessary as the battery was placed specially at the disposal of the 51st (Highland) Division for the attack, and received its orders during the engagement direct from the Artillery Commander of that division, and of the Guards Division which relieved it.

The greatest difficulty encountered in moving warfare arises from transport problems. Except in very dry weather, F.W.D.'s and lorries cannot leave the hard road, the guns must be pulled into and out of position by the exertions of their detachments. Sometimes, when in difficulties, we have received assistance from one of the larger types of tractors, a " caterpillar," or even a passing " tank," but man power is usually the main and only method employed.

There is no reserve of lorries beyond the number stated, which is only sufficient to carry the ammunition allotment and stores. Any breakdown of a lorry increases the difficulties, therefore, and necessitates a double journey, some of the transport returning to the old position to pick up stores left behind. Unless extra lorries are detailed by higher authority for the transport of the personnel these have to march, as there is no room for them in the lorries when all the essential stores are packed. The stores referred to may roughly be described as follows:—

Spare gun stores,
Artificer's tools,
Wheeler's tools,
Spare wheels for guns and limbers,
Signalling stores (lamps, flags, cable, poles, instruments, etc.,
Wireless installation,
Battery Commander's stores (maps, optical instruments, etc.),
Stores of clothing and equipment,
Officers' and men's kits,
Cookhouse stoves and stores,
Supply of reserve rations,

and last, but not least, 450 rounds of ammunition, this last item being 27 tons in weight. The weight of a gun and limber is 5½ tons, and the tractor which pulls it is not supposed to carry more than 30 cwts.

CHAPTER II.

EARLY DAYS.

On 17th November, 1916, under Authority W.O. 20 (Artillery) 3816 (A.G. 6), dated 17/11/16, the 303rd Siege Battery, R.G.A., was formed at Crown Hill, Plymouth. The establishment was to be that laid down on page 10 of pamphlet S.D. 2, dated 10/8/16, for a battery armed with 6″ B.L. How., Authority R.G.A. Records, A98/734.

The Battery started its existence under the temporary command of 2nd Lieut. G. C. Woods, assisted by B.S.M. Back and B.Q.M.S. Jeffs, but after a few days Lieut. Woods handed over to 2nd Lieut. S. B. Castle, and B.Q.M.S. Jeffs to B.Q.M.S. Carr. On 18th December, 2nd Lieut. A. R. Landale joined, and his seniority placed him at the head of affairs. Meantime batches of men were being posted from various batteries, companies, or schools, and by the beginning of the New Year training was in full swing under Sergts. Gillott, Tanner, Legge, and Meadows. During the first three days of January three other officers joined—2nd Lieuts. E. G. Silverton, C. H. Ledward, and P. W. Scott. The last-named was transferred to 299th Siege Battery before we left England.

On 15th January we moved to Ewshott, where Capt. W. T. Saidler joined us from the York R.G.A., and took command. Here we chiefly recollect the bitter frosts which froze the canal and our water supply (thus supplying us with excellent skating and making washing an almost unobtainable luxury). Part of our work, as usual, consisted of digging gun pits—the standard pattern of which we have never since had the misfortune to see. Following the prevailing fashion we had a battery photograph taken, thus providing ourselves with our first " souvenir."

On 2nd February we marched to Aldershot, where the officers were lodged in the Marlborough Lines Mess, and the men in the Tournay Barracks. Here most of us saw a 6″ 26-cwt. Howitzer for the first time, and made the acquaintance, equipped with P. H. helmets, of the " gas chamber." Measles were raging in the barracks at this time, and thereby we lost Mr. Scott and 38 men, none of whom returned to us. On 14th February B.S.M. Back was posted R.S.M. of the 87th H.A. Group, and was replaced by B.S.M. Steel.

On 26th February, a wearisome train journey brought us to Hut Town, Lydd. Our "shooting practices" did not make much of a stir in I.G. circles, but Mr. Silverton's previous experience proved of great value. On 2nd March we had the honour of being inspected by Field Marshal Sir J. French. On 8th March, Capt. Graham became our Commanding Officer, but on the 12th he was transfered to 301st Siege Battery, on the appointment of Major H. W. Lockhart, who joined us ultimately at Larkhill on the 29th.

Our final home station was Larkhill (No. 27 Camp), whither we moved on 15th March. Here we had the misfortune to have our first casualties, Bombardier Partington dying of appendicitis and Gunner Townsend of cerebro-spinal meningitis. Our time was fully occupied in drawing, issuing, and sorting mobilisation stores, and going on and returning from overseas leave. Some of us had the unpleasant experience of being recalled for a "practice mobilisation," but by the end of the month all preparations had been completed, and we were ready to " proceed overseas."

CHAPTER III.

THE BATTERY PROCEEDS OVERSEAS.

At last the time had arrived for the battery to proceed overseas and take its place as an Active Service unit.

On the 1st April an advance party left for France, and the following day the main body marched out of camp under the command of Major H. W. L. Lockhart, the new O.C., who had been posted to the battery.

Our journey was begun at 7.30 a.m., when we left Larkhill for Amesbury Station, entraining there at 8.45 a.m. A heavy snowstorm marked our departure. Southampton was reached at 11 a.m., and at 4.30 p.m., after a dreary wait, we embarked on the s.s. "Londonderry."

Nothing of an unusual nature took place in the crossing, other than some temporary unhappiness occasioned by the rough seas, and the very wonderful degree of security that has been maintained throughout the war in the Channel crossings was accorded to us. After a long night Le Havre was reached at 5.30 a.m. on the 3rd April, and having disembarked we marched to the Docks Rest Camp there. Here a junction was made with the advance party, who, however, left again the following day for the battle area.

After a few days' rest, instructions were received for us to move, and having put the guns aboard, we entrained and left Le Havre at 3 o'clock on the afternoon of 8th April.

The first journey up the line has always memories for those who made it, and while our journey did not materially differ from all the others that have been made, it left vivid impressions. The first stage occupied some thirty-three hours, and just before its completion the battery were given their first glimpse of what was afterwards to become their normal experience. Viewed from the train, gun flashes could distinctly be seen lighting up the night, and a hush came over all of us as the intimate knowledge and realisation of the part we were about to take thus unfolded itself.

Arriving at Bailleul the guns were detrained, and billets found for the night at the Y.M.C.A. hut there. After twelve hours' rest a start was made for Dranoutre, near which our first position was to be located.

It may be useful here to recall the operations in progress when we first became an active service unit.

As a result of the autumn campaign upon the Somme in 1916, the British troops held the high ground in that area. Efforts were now being made to extend these gains farther North, and whilst we were journeying up the line the battle for Vimy Ridge had been fought, thus extending our hold between Arras and Lens.

Although this had not been accomplished, when we received orders to take up a position it was evidently with the object of taking part in a further projected attack on the same ridge running out in the direction of Ypres.

We were attached to the 23rd H.A.G. of the 9th Corps, 2nd Army.

Arriving on our position, tents were put up to serve as billets. These were pitched in a newly ploughed field, the condition of which, softened by successive frost, snow, and rain, will be well remembered by those who were with us then, and easily imagined by those who were not. Strenuous and persistent work improved the drainage to some extent, although the weather remained persistently cold and wet until the end of April.

Work was immediately started on the battery position. Gun emplacements, shell and cartridge recesses, and trenches were dug, and it was on the 13th April, whilst engaged on this work, that we had our first experience of being under shell fire. By the 19th the work was well advanced, and we got three guns into position. The following day we opened fire. Our first target was necessarily one for registration and calibration. Later other targets were engaged, and the 20th April has to be recorded as the opening date for our active participation in the war.

During the remaining days of April we did much work to improve our billets. There was some enemy shelling, to which we replied with great vigour. It was in this period that we carried out our first aeroplane shoot, and we also had to carry out a prolonged bombardment programme, when we fired four hundred rounds on the Dammstrasse ; a very notable target at that time.

One of the guns went out of action owing to mechanical fault. This was the forerunner of much gun trouble. From now onwards we were constantly having to send one or more of our guns to workshops for repairs, and these difficulties did not cease until some time after we got to Ypres.

On the opening day of May we suffered our first casualties, Gnr. G. Stewart was killed when carrying rations from the billets to the battery, and Sig. Matheson was wounded later in the day whilst on duty on the position.

A period of heavy firing now ensued, including quite a good shoot with balloon observation. Our guns were kept busy until the 7th May, when the gun troubles became acute, and we were temporarily put out of action pending their repair.

One of the quite infrequent attempts to hold a religious service had been made on the 6th May, but it was not allowed to proceed without interruption. " Battery Action" was given whilst the service was in progress, and, as it turned out, very fortunately so, for almost immediately a shell came over and burst in the very pit we had just vacated.

We were now becoming more accustomed, not only to war conditions, but also to the new life of a foreign country. We received from the Flemish peasantry an excellent welcome. The alarms of war and its close proximity had failed to drive them away from their homes. We found that, almost without exception, the Flemish language was spoken in this district, and, although so near to the French frontier, the language of their neighbours was rarely employed. The peasantry had, however, become wonderfully well acquainted with English during the war, including some of the less choice phrasings of our tongue. The battery dietary could be pleasantly augmented by purchasing meals at the cottages, the prices charged being extremely moderate, and especially so when contrasted with the extortionate sums demanded at later times on other parts of the front. It may be interesting to recall that a supper of coffee, with milk and sugar, bread, butter, and a couple of eggs, could be obtained for seven pence.

Whilst the guns were out of action we were employed in laying light railways for bringing up ammunition for ourselves and prospective batteries. We did much hard work in laying wooden rails, but unfortunately this system proved faulty in use, and shortly afterwards we had to replace them with iron ones.

By the 12th May, our guns having been repaired and brought back, we were again in action. The days and nights that followed were marked by continuous work. The firing orders were heavy, and it was found necessary to construct more suitable shelters at the battery position which would afford better protection, and also greater space and comfort.

In addition to the daily ammunition requirements, orders were received to accumulate four thousand rounds on the position. As many as a thousand rounds were received in one night. We managed to complete the dump by the 25th May. There was a good deal of hostile shelling at this time, a considerable proportion being gas.

In review, the month of May was an exceedingly strenuous one for the battery, comprising as it did the laying and relaying of light railway lines, the construction of dug-outs and shelters, and constant shell humping. We were fortunate, however, in escaping without further casualty beyond those already recorded, except that Sergt. Meadows was accidently injured whilst helping to remedy a defect in one of the guns. Some, too, had been unable to stand the strain and had gone down the line as the result of sickness, whilst reinforcements had been sent to replace them.

Meanwhile great activities were going on around us in preparation for the projected attack on the Messines Ridge. Many batteries pulled into position in our neighbourhood with guns of all calibres. The accumulation of artillery was greater than had been used in the battle for Vimy Ridge, of which this effort in which we were to take part was a continuation.

Unfortunately our guns were still giving great trouble, and when the opening bombardment began only "B" gun remained serviceable. This gun, however, did excellent work, firing continuously day and night from the 3rd June up to the morning of the great attack.

We were occasionally harassed by enemy fire during this bombardment, and had a few cases of slight gassing.

With the first streaks of dawn on the 7th June the massed guns opened out. At no time previously had there been so great a concentration of artillery fire upon so limited an area. Our one gun did well, the detachments on duty under Sergt. Legge and Cpl. Douglas as No.'s 1 firing 350 rounds.

In addition to the artillery fire some twenty mines which had been driven into the Messines-Wytchaete Ridge were simultaneously exploded, resulting in the formation of the great Messines Crater. So great was the noise of these explosions that it was distinctly heard across the Channel, while to those who were there it was absolutely deafening, the whole countryside shaking with the reverberations.

Our signalling section had throughout especially heavy duties in repairing the lines, which were constantly being broken. On one occasion the Group line had gone, and Sigs. Mottershead and McFarlane were detailed to go out and repair it. Knowing the at once risky nature of the work, and the urgent necessity for communication being re-established, the O.C., with grim humour, added to the order: "Tell them there is a D.C.M. if they mend it and a D.C.M. if they don't." We have no record of any award, but the line was successfullly repaired. In this connection "Daylight Corner" will long be remembered by our signallers.

Very shortly after the opening of the bombardment on the morning of the attack 2nd Lieut. E. G. Silverton and a party of signallers went forward to reconnoitre, at the same time attempting to maintain communication with the battery by means of helio. This system did not work satisfactorily owing to the great number of other parties similarly engaged; Mr. Silverton was slightly wounded, but remained on duty. Sig. S. N. Miller was also detailed to accompany the heavy artillery liaison officer along with telephonists from other units. This party having spent the night in the support trenches, went forward at daybreak and maintained communications, throughout the successive stages of the battle, between the infantry and the artillery. It may be mentioned that Sig. Miller went to the extreme point reached that day, remaining with the officer throughout his tour of duty.

After firing the bombardment tasks our share in the Battle of Messines was completed, apart from some few targets at extreme range.

The objective tried for in this action was a limited one, and was successfully achieved. It was considered to have proved definitely that, supported by massed artillery, our infantry could gain any objective, no matter what troops were opposed to them.

The following day, after the heights overlooking the country towards Ypres had become definitely ours, we made preparations for leaving, and at half-past eight on the evening of 8th June we marched out of camp to Vlammertinghe, in the Ypres sector.

Upon our arrival there close on midnight, we halted at the cross roads in that village. It was a very deadly spot for such a halt, but we were happily ignorant of the danger. Here we were relieved of the two guns we had brought with us, which were immediately needed for 168th Siege Battery, while we ourselves were put on board passing motor lorries and sent back. The destination of these lorries turned out to be the Siege Park on the Proven Road, and here for a few hours we got a much needed and welcome rest.

During this short respite the pleasing news was received that, pending the arrival of other guns, we were to have a rest.

Taking the road again we marched the next day to Houtkerque, crossing the frontier from Belgium to France.

This proved to be a very delightful break for us. We were billeted at Sileneau Farm, a spacious farmhouse which, with adjoining barns, paddocks and meadows provided quarters for the officers, billets for the men, and means of recreation for all.

The genial weather, coupled with the country fare which we could purchase most reasonably, did much towards recuperating our flagging energies, and proved an excellent preparation for the stern times ahead. We were for the first time amongst a French-speaking population, who were without even the smattering of English acquired by the peasantry at Dranoutre. This, however, did not prove an unsurmountable barrier, and cordial relations were soon established with our temporary neighbours.

Preparations for our next position had to be made, and on the 12th June 2nd Lieut. C. H. Ledward and thirty other ranks went on as an advance party to Ypres, which was to be the scene of action.

Three days later the remainder of the battery followed, making the journey by motor lorry to Vlammertinghe, where billets had been secured.

Vlammertinghe, as will be remembered, is about 3½ miles almost due West of Ypres: it was at one time a pleasant farming and fruit-growing area, but when we arrived there it had suffered considerably from shell fire. The church by the cross roads was badly damaged, the spire having evidently been used as a registration point for German artillery, and the cross roads were a point to which special attention was given. The civil population had gone, but many of the houses still remained intact, and the village made a convenient billeting area for troops coming out of Ypres. Compared with that city Vlammertinghe seemed a very haven of refuge. Our administrative headquarters and stores were located there, telephonic communication being established with the battery.

The battery position was in the city of Ypres itself. For 2½ years some of the most desperate struggles had been fought there, and, though placed, as it was, in the centre of a salient, successive and persistent attempts had failed to dislodge our forces from this pivotal stronghold.

We were attached to the 19th Corps of the 5th Army. For administrative purposes we were placed in the 23rd H.A.G., but received our tactical instructions from the 9th H.A.G.

The advance party had already commenced work on the battery position, which was sited in and about a stable yard and slaughter house between the Prison and the historic " Place" of the City. We were thus quite close to what had at one time been the Cloth Hall, famous in the annals of Flemish industry, and also to the Cathedral of which only the broken walls and partially demolished tower remained. With the grim irony of war we were but a hundred yards, too, from the Plaine d'Amour, and whatever scenes had once occasioned such a title it now sadly belied its name.

Work on the making of shell and cardridge recesses was pressed forward. From the nature of the ground it was impossible to construct dug-outs, so " elephant iron" sections had to be employed. These were placed inside such buildings as were standing, and being further covered with bricks, provided most substantial shelters.

Whilst engaged on this work we lost Sergt. Gillott and Gnrs. Hitchin and Dobbs, who were wounded and sent to hospital. Later we were sorry to know that Sergt. Gillott, who was both our youngest and senior sergeant, had lost his arm.

The two guns which were in workshops when we left Dranoutre were now returned to us, and two more were lent by 279th Siege Battery. We got these four guns into position, and were ready for action by the 22nd June, and commenced firing on that date. This new complement of guns did not prove much more satisfactory than our former ones, and we had considerable mechanical troubles to deal with, which were made yet more troublesome by the extremely dangerous position we were in.

Indeed, a description of this period would be little more than a diary of misfortune. There were so few British batteries then in the line that we felt we were the only battery to bear the brunt, and seemed quite powerless effectively to reply to the constant shelling; each night, too, from 500 to a 1,000 rounds of ammunition came up, and these had to be unloaded, usually under shell fire. We did not expend this number, but so much was destroyed that one daily duty was to count how much had been lost during the previous night.

Our journeys between the position and the billets by lorry were too full of excitement to be pleasant, whilst Vlammertingne itself was anything but free from shelling. On one occasion a part of the billets was wrecked, Gnr. Hill, the storeman, being killed.

The following extracts from 2nd Lieut. Ledward's diary might be interesting as illustrating the succession of events. Mr. Ledward was particularly in a position to record such happenings; he acted as Section Officer, remaining for sixteen consecutive days in the battery position :—

23rd June.—Cookhouse three times buried. In firing 20 rounds two guns went out of action ; 900 rounds of gas fell near.

24th June.—A better day; fired 10 to 20 rounds on each of 12 targets, finishing with aeroplane shoot.

25th June.—"Eight inch" shoot on battery; one gun hit; one casualty (Mr. Ruffel).

26th and 27th June.—Attempted aeroplane shoot stopped by hostile shelling and gun trouble.

28th June.—No guns left.

The casualties during this period were :—

2nd Lieut. S. B. Castle and 2nd Lieut. W G. Ruffel, both of whom were wounded and went to hospital.

Actg. Bmdr. Potter, slightly wounded; Gnr. Hornby, Gnr. Toone, Gnr. Alexander, Gnr. Hodgkinson, wounded and to hospital.

It very soon became apparent that if we were to carry on as an effective unit it was necessary to find a position less subject to enemy fire. The City of Ypres was continually under fire, and even when this fire was not directed against ourselves it materially interfered with successful work.

A new position was therefore chosen, some five hundred yards away on our left flank near the Canal. Work was commenced here on the

29th June, and carried forward to the 7th July. During this period of transition we did very little firing, our energies being concentrated on making our new quarters. These promised to be more healthy for us than the old ones, and, the enemy being unaware of the change for some time after it was made, we had the comforting satisfaction of seeing him continue to shell our old position after we had left it.

By the morning of the 7th July we had our four guns in the new position, but with the long tale of casualties our numbers were so reduced that we could only muster sufficient to man three of them.

Quite the worst experience we had gone through up to this time occurred on the evening of 6th July; while preparing to move our last gun, a single stray shell coming over killed Cpl. Jukes and wounded nineteen others.

Despite our losses, a shoot with aeroplane observation was carried out on the 7th July; so successful was this shoot that the Brigadier-General sent us a special congratulatory message.

There was an intention at this time to increase our establishment to that of a six-gun battery, and a section of 371st Siege Battery, which had recently come overseas, was sent from the Base to join us for that purpose.

This party consisted of 2nd Lieut. J. N. Green and 57 other ranks. So far, however, from adding to our previous establishment, they simply served to provide sufficient numbers to man our four guns and allow for relief detachments.

These reinforcements did not have any better fortune than had fallen to us; within two days of their arrival casualties occurred amongst them. On the 10th July we were subjected to a destructive shoot; very little material damage was done, and when the shoot was apparently over the detachments on duty went for tea. These mainly consisted of the new reinforcements. Whilst they were at the cookhouse a 5'9 burst amongst them killing Gnrs. Cleator, McFarlane, and Berry, and wounding four others. This disaster was followed the same evening by another; actg. Bmdr. Hancocks and Gnr. Oswald, whilst on their way to billets, were wounded, the latter so severely that he died the next day.

In this position we had dug-outs driven into the Canal bank. These were fairly sound and proof against the lighter calibre shelling; they were, however, the scene of further losses.

It was at this time that the Germans first began to use yellow cross or mustard gas. On the 12th July, Ypres and district were subjected to an intense area bombardment with it.

Great activity was being manifested amongst our forces at this time; large movements amongst the infantry were taking place, and they suffered along with the artillery.

The gas bombardment started about 10 o'clock at night, and lasted for about five hours; the shells used were principally of small calibre, but they simply showered on us.

The effects of the gas were not immediately noticeable, and we were caught somewhat unawares. The detachments were scattered in the various dug-outs, and whilst the bombardment lasted it was well-nigh impossible to communicate with them.

With the dawn the attack ceased, and the early rising sun broke through warm and bright upon a pitiable spectacle. No fewer than 56 of our men were suffering from the effects of the gas, and in addition Gnr. Pickett had been killed. To add to our immediate diffi-culties we received orders to fire twenty rounds on a given target before 6 o'clock, and it was no easy matter to find sufficient men to carry this out. Curiously enough a large number of the section of 371st Battery that had joined us were again amongst the sufferers.

The effects of this gas, which was quite new in warfare, pro-duced loss of voice and physical power, inflammation of the eyes, and sores breaking out on the body.

On the 16th July the preliminary bombardment on the German trenches and positions began ; this was the opening offensive move-ment in the Third Battle of Ypres. The object was to obtain possession of the ridges lying to the North and East of Ypres, which overlook the city.

We were allotted the task of firing on the network of protective trenches and wire entanglements ; we had also to fire on various strong points. For a week this bombardment continued, our own ammunition expenditure being nearly 4,000 rounds, with quite good results.

When, however, the date fixed for the attack came along, it was found that the results expected from the bombardment had not been sufficiently achieved. The shooting had been largely " blind," and the German defences were considered to be still too strong ; it was therefore decided to prolong the artillery preparation by another week.

During these bombardments several changes took place in the battery ; Capt. W. T. Saidler left for 16th Corps Heavy Artillery, and 2nd Lieut. A. R. Landale rejoined us. In connection with Capt. Saidler's change it may be added that he later transferred to the Flying Corps, and unhappily was killed the following November. On the 20th July Major H. W. Lockhart, who had been in command during the overseas service of the battery, was now posted as O.C. 51st H.A.G. He was succeeded by Major E. H. Huxford, M.C., from 49th Siege Battery.

When Major Huxford came to the battery he was already suffer-ing from the effects of gas, and after being in command for three days he was compelled to relinquish his duties and go to hospital. Although his stay at this time was so short, he impressed himself upon the battery by his very determined attempt to extinguish some blazing ammunition that had been fired by enemy shelling. Bmdr. Putt also displayed great daring and resource at this time, and was subse-quently awarded the Military Medal in recognition of his work. This was the first decoration granted in the battery.

The amount of ammunition lost in this manner was very con-siderable, and made the work of checking it very difficult. As an instance, when we left our first position in Ypres we had there some 2,500 rounds, but before it could be salved so much had been de-stroyed that not one-tenth of it was retrieved complete.

Actg. Capt. Silverton succeeded Major Huxford as O.C. but he was not destined to hold the position long, as he was unfortunately killed on the 26th July during a bombardment of the battery area, a 5'9 H.E. shell bursting on the side of the dug-out used as the command post, killing the O.C. and wounding 2nd Lieut. Grieg and Gnr. Hollingworth, the B.C.A. on duty. Gnr. Hollingworth died the following day in hospital. We had also several cases of shell-shock, gassing, and slightly wounded, which made further inroads on our numbers and made the manning of the guns a serious problem.

Capt. A. J. Steward was next posted as O.C., coming from 27th Siege Battery, and joined on the evening of 26th July. That same evening Mr .Landale, who was suffering from gas, had to go off duty, and went to hospital the next day.

There were now only two officers available for duty, the new O.C. and Mr. Ledward, who, together, had to face the direction of the heavy firing tasks allotted to us in the prolonged bombardment. Later Mr. Green, who had been temporarily lent to 27th Siege Battery, returned and took his share of the work.

After the disaster in the command post the dug-outs along the Canal bank were abandoned, and other shelters found a short distance from this too well-marked spot. This change was hastened by three 12″ shells bursting between the dug-outs. Fortunately no one was injured, although Cpl. Price had a remarkably narrow escape. Our new dug-outs in construction offered no better protection than those we had left, but they happily served us quite well.

From the 28th July our fire increased in intensity, and on the 30th July we fired 988 rounds, which for a long time was our record number, and, indeed, was never surpassed while we remained a four-gun battery.

On the 31st July the attack was launched. We opened out at 3.50 a.m., firing in the barage programme. The weather militated against complete success; it was both wet and tempestuous, hampering the infantry and retarding the Tanks, and thus gave time for strong counter-attacks to be developed.

A gain of a few thousand yards was the net result on our front, and as far as we were concerned proved to be very useful. Being still in range of such targets as we were required to fire on, we did not follow up, and reaped the advantage of being less subject to enemy shelling, as the German artillery had necessarily to be drawn further back.

During this battle we had only one casualty; Gnr. Lambert, who formed one of the Forward Observation Officer's party, failed to return, and was later reported wounded.

In the early days of August we had repeatedly to respond to S.O.S. calls; on the 3rd we expended nearly 400 rounds on these targets alone. Our weary and jaded gun teams were never too tired to respond to these calls with alacrity. There is no call for " battery action " which electrifies artillerymen into activity so much as the call for S.O.S. And at this time, when our numbers were so seriously depleted that the same detachments had to remain continuously on duty, there was no failure in maintaining this tradition.

Preparations were made for a more advanced position, a new one being selected N.E. of the village of St. Jean. Digging parties went forward and did much work under difficult conditions. They were very speedily spotted by the enemy, and constantly subjected to bursts of fire.

Reinforcements now arrived from the Base, and two officers, 2nd Lieut. Ainscough and 2nd Lieut .Guttery, also joined the battery on the 5th August. We were, however, much below strength, and we were further reduced by a "premature" occurring on our No. 3 gun on the 6th August. Eight n.c.o.'s and men were wounded as a result, including Sergt. Blake, who subsequently died in hospital. The piece was completely wrecked, and the following day our No. 2 gun was hit by a gas shell, which broke the trail; this left us with two guns in action. We were shortly afterwards supplied with two new guns from Ordnance, which proved much more satisfactory in use than anything we had previously been equipped with. Another "premature" occurred on 21st August. This time, however, the shell had already left the piece before bursting, and the gun was un-damaged, and, although several of the men on duty were hit, their injuries were fortunately so slight that none had to be removed to hospital.

On the 10th August B.Q.M.S. Carr left us to become Actg. B.S.M. of 116th Siege Battery. He had been with the battery almost from its formation, and left with the good wishes of all. At a later date we were pleased to learn that he had been given a commission. Cpl. Bennet temporarily assumed the duties of Quartermaster-Sergeant until relieved by the posting of B.Q.M.S. Munro to the battery.

Other changes also occurred; Capt. Steward was promoted Major on the 15th August, but that same day developed symptoms of trench fever, and the day following went to hospital, thus termina-ting his short connection with the battery; Mr. Green, who had been promoted Actg. Capt., became O.C., and remained in command until the arrival from the 1st Army of Capt. W. D. Bennett on the 26th August; 2nd Lieut. W. Bloye had arrived from the Base the previous day; Mr. Ledward, who throughout the many changes had so far escaped, now had an attack of trench fever. Happily this attack did not sever his connection with the battery although he was unable to participate in its activities for some months to come.

Cheering rumours now began to circulate amongst us; rumour is always busy but often false. This time, however, there was a more convincing note in what we heard, which was to the effect that we were to have a change to a quieter sector.

In truth we needed it. For months we had seen our ranks con-tinually being depleted, reinforced, and depleted again. The long hours on duty, the incessant shelling, the perilous journeys between the positions and the billets, together with the periodic night bomb-ing, had left marks on the hardiest. The prospect was therefore a welcome one, and with the coming of September it was definitely settled that we were to exchange positions, guns, and stores with 119th Siege Battery.

At once preparations were begun for the change; the stores were all checked, and such as we had to take with us were separated.

These latter stores were quite considerable. Although we had never been equipped with more than four guns, our establishment was nominally that of a six-gun battery; consequently we had surplus stores for two guns, which were not handed over to our successors.

No record of our stay in the Ypres sector would be complete without a tribute to the relaxation that was afforded by the near proximity of Poperinghe.

Although comparatively so near to the war zone it maintained itself as a bright and bustling township; the constant stream of motor lorries afforded us a speedy if irregular means of transport from Vlammertinghe. In Poperinghe we could obtain a bath and change, which gave some temporary relief from the too insistent attentions of what " Mr. Punch" has discreetly named "the fauna of the trenches." One could also buy a meal at any of the numerous restaurants, the staple fare being fried eggs, potatoes, and salad, with coffee. More daring patrons would boldly call for beefsteak, although whether their orders were exactly executed is open to question. The cinema houses, divisional concert parties, the Talbot House, and kindred institutions all provided a pleasant diversion from the sterner happenings at Ypres.

CHAPTER IV.

RECONSTRUCTION.

Preparations for the exchange of positions and stores with 119th Siege Battery were now well advanced, and during the morning of 3rd September one section of that battery arrived and were shortly being made acquainted with their new surroundings. Later in the day our Right Section, having handed over their duties to the new detachments, left for Poperinghe.

The following day, Tuesday, 4th Sept., Major J. O. K. Delap from 216th Siege Battery ,joined as O.C., and this date is marked as inaugurating a new and distinctive era in our history; happily by his coming the long succession of changes in command now terminated. These changes, together with our many casualties, had naturally resulted in some disorganisation in the work, and a lack of settled system in administration. Such internal difficulties were now very shortly remedied, and uniform methods evolved.

The command of the joint battery was definitely assumed by 119th Siege Battery on the 5th September, an aeroplane shoot being carried out that same afternoon.

Our Right Section were undeniably glad to shake the dust of Ypres from their feet. This, it may be added, was one of the few occasions in that wet summer when such action was possible. Normally we were encrusted with mud; the thick and heavy clay seemed especially adapted for its production. The well-earned rest which the section had been accorded was not allowed to be unbroken. During the first night an enemy plane bombed the town of Poperinghe, one bomb falling on the outbuilding of our rest billets and wounding Gnr. Gill, who was outside at the time, so severely that he died the next day.

The journey to our new position was made in three separate sections; the Right and Left Sections, which proceeded by train, and the Transport Party, which travelled by road.

The Transport Party was the first to get away, and left Vlammertinghe in the early evening of 6th September. An exceedingly heavy thunderstorm marked the departure; a halt was made at the Siege Park, Poperinghe. It was an intensely black night, and while the darkness and the rain freed the party from the risk of being bombed, there were some little untoward happenings as the result. More than one member of the party found himself floundering in the mud of the trenches which served to drain the park. These small troubles were soon forgotten in the genial warmth of the succeeding day, the journey being resumed about noon.

Passing through Hazebrouck and Armentieres, we reached Bethune in the evening, where the lorries were parked for the night. Arrangements for billeting were made at the permanent barracks.

These promised to be more commodious than comfortable. A very casual inspection revealed "a certain liveliness," and it was considered advisable to return to the more tranquil if cooler lorries.

Arras was reached by mid-day, and presented a rather less battered appearance than was noticeable when we again passed through a year later. In the early evening we arrived at Bief Villiers, and after spending the night there went forward to Metz-en-Couture, which was the nearest village to our new positions. Here a junction was made with the Right Section, which had already arrived.

They had travelled by train and had passed through the northern part of the Somme battle area.

On the 17th September our Left Section, having been relieved by the remaining section of 119th Siege Battery, left the position at Ypres and proceeded to Poperinghe for a brief rest. Whilst here a football match was arranged with 281st Siege Battery, resulting in a win for our team.

The change to the 3rd Army being thus effected, we proceeded to establish ourselves in Havrincourt Wood, temporarily taking over the bivouacs and shelters vacated by 119th Siege Battery. These were immediately near to the gun positions. We found the working of the battery to be sectional, and as the distance between the sections was about a mile, they were at first controlled separately, with a command post at either section, following the system used by the outgoing battery.

There followed a period necessarily devoted to training and reconstruction. The casualties suffered by the battery at Ypres had necessitated the posting of reinforcements from many different sources; sometimes, when things were at their worst men had been sent to us from other batteries in the line; others had come out to us from England in drafts, and from Base Depôts in France. The battery was very short of specialists, and men had to be trained for the special duties of B.C.A.'s Observers, Aeroplane Spotters, Layers, etc. Added to this, the officers had suffered many changes. Our new O.C. was actually the seventh to take command of the battery. Our Captain, although an experienced officer, was new to the battery, and several of the junior officers had had little experience of active service. It is one of the difficulties of the heavy artillery that, being always in the line, they have to do their training while in action; and in our case this disability was greatly felt at this time.

We were fortunate in having been sent to a quiet front, in taking over prepared positions, and in the summer weather; but the firing programme allotted to us had to be maintained at all costs. We were further helped by the fact that, though we had only four guns, our personnel was nominally that of a six-gun battery. This enabled us to have a certain number of men detached from firing duty each day for the purpose of training.

Classes were immediately set on foot to train the various specialists required. Amongst others the B.C.A.'s class was started, attended by Bmdrs. Trotter and Miller and Gnr. Beardsworth (who has, in his time, usefully filled almost every appointment in the battery), and later by Cpl. Bird when he rejoined. This proved of the utmost value, the n.c.o.'s concerned taking the keenest interest in their duties, and it may be here remarked that the B.C.A.'s who began at this period, supplemented later by Bmdr. Birrell, carried out the exacting and responsible work of Battery Commander's Assistants until the end of the war.

On our arrival we came under the 14th H.A. Group (Col. Rowan Robinson), but shortly afterwards were taken over by the 29th H.A. Group, then commanded by Col. Macalpine-Leny, D.S.O.

During the first month the weather was generally fine and warm, with just a touch of frost at night to remind us that winter was approaching. This was, perhaps, the most tranquil period the battery ever enjoyed during its active service, and the open life contrasting so strongly with our recent experiences did much to restore the general tone of the personnel. The fields surrounding were ablaze with poppies, and the scarlet pimpernel could be found growing around our dug-outs.

These arcadian environments, pleasant as they were while the weather remained good, promised poor protection for the winter months, and as it seemed likely that we were more or less permanently established, preparations were immediately begun on more substantial quarters. These were selected with a view to their being a central control for the guns, administrative headquarters for the battery, and winter billets for the whole of the personnel.

The site chosen lay roughly midway between the two positions, and the buildings, though now in ruins, had no doubt once been a prosperous farmstead on the outskirts of Metz. Every advantage was taken, in planning the billets, of what still remained standing. The officers' quarters, command post, battery office, telephone exchange, guard room, artificer's and wheeler's workshops and canteen were all ranged around what had formerly been the courtyard. Nissen huts were obtained and erected in the orchard and paddock adjoining. These were allotted to the sub-sections, the B.Q.M.S., and the Signalling Section. The whole was connected by a system of pathways with duckboards below and camouflage above. Everything was done to conceal us from aerial observation, and, when completed, formed a most compact arrangement of winter quarters. The sergeants established a separate mess in adjacent premises.

The map room, which was also the central command post, was quite a model of its kind. The walls were hung with the most recent counter-battery and enemy organisation maps; our own fighting map was conveniently placed so as to ensure the targets being quickly determined for either gun section; and telephonic communication was established with all stations.

The scheme of these billets also included the construction of deep and commodious dug-outs, and a considerable amount of constructional work was carried out during the months of October and November on these projects.

At this time we were joined by 2nd Lieut. Austin Y. Hoy, an American citizen, who had volunteered for service with the British Army from a desire to get into the scrap as soon as possible. He was posted away to another battery in about a month, and we were sorry to lose him.

Several other officers joined the battery during the autumn months, including 2nd Lieut. J. Bleese and 2nd Lieut. G. A. Smith, who was attached to us from the R.F.A. Later, 2nd Lieut. B. W. Yardley, 2nd Lieut S. A. R. Farrell, 2nd Lieut. R. W. Grindley, and 2nd Lieut. W. C. N. F. Dobb joined us on various dates ; but with the exception of Mr Yardley, who remained with us throughout, these were only temporary attachments.

Our gun positions were so well concealed, and the precautions taken to avoid detection so thorough, that throughout the whole of September and the early days of October we were comparatively free from hostile shelling, and such as did occur fortunately caused no casualties. The only occasion worthy of record was during the third week in September, when the Left Section had an uncomfortable time owing to heavy shelling to their rear. Work on the billets had to be temporarily suspended, as the result of a prolonged destructive shoot on a field battery that had pulled in close to. It is interesting to record that, while our neighbours suffered much material damage, they fortunately escaped without casualty. Subsequently they moved to another position, and thus ceased to attract to us these unwelcome attentions.

Our long immunity was not to be maintained, and on the 10th October our Right Section was subjected to a very thorough destructive shoot by a 5.9 Howitzer Battery. They opened out on us at 8.30 a.m., and from the first they were well on their target. The shelling continued, with short breaks, until 2.30 p.m., by which time they had pretty completely achieved their purpose. Both gun pits were smashed up, No. 1 gun had two direct hits, one of which burst right in the muzzle, with the effect of so contorting the nose of the piece that it largely resembled the widened end of a gramophone trumpet. No. 2 pit was empty at the time, the gun having been taken to workshops for repair. Happily there were no casualties, but the position was rendered quite untenable. It is interesting to recall that this was the first day that Mr. Hoy, who was the Section Officer on duty, had undertaken such work since joining the battery, and that two days later, when he was taking duty at the Left Section, that position was also shelled for the first time, fortunately without effect. This so worked on the poor man's mind that great difficulty was experienced in persuading him that he was not a " Jonah."

Our own shooting during this time was of a very general nature. The targets allotted were principally counter-battery work, together with harassing fire on trench systems, roads, railways, and canal bridges. We carried out some very successful destructive shoots on enemy batteries with both aeroplane and ground observation.

One of the most notable of these targets was a destructive shoot on a nest of trench mortar batteries that had been located at Boggart's Hole, on the western edge of Havrincourt Chateau grounds and south of the village of Havrincourt. This nest had been most troublesome and we were ordered to suppress their activities.

In order to observe more closely the effect of our fire, Major Delap, accompanied by Mr. Ledward and Mr. Green, with Sig. Stott as telephonist, went forward and secured a point of vantage in the

THE RIGHT SECTION BEHIND HAVRINCOURT WOOD (Air Photograph).

The arrow points between the gun positions and indicates the "centre line." The shell holes seen are those made by the 4·2 gun which shelled the position at intervals, and are not those of the 5·9 howitzer which did the "destructive shoot" on the position.

front line. Major Delap conducted the shoot, and the result was entirely successful. At the beginning of the shoot an attempt was made with first charge in order to secure the greater angle of descent, but it did not prove steady enough at that range, and a change was made to second charge, which at once gave effective results. The nest was completely silenced, and the principal offender, which had been dubbed " Peter," did not fire again. On this same occasion two other targets were engaged, one being a company H.Q., and the other a concrete O.P. The first was destroyed, and the second, which was seen to be in use, was badly damaged.

As already stated, the destructive shoot which had been carried out on our Right Section necessitated a change in position, and a fresh site was selected on the Gouzeaucourt Road, about half a mile from the billets. Work on this new position was commenced on 20th October, and eight days later, after being much hampered by broken weather, the Section was again in action. The position chosen was an excellent one. Our gun pits were dug into the banked roadside and roofed with corrugated steel supported on wide girders. The top was turfed and planted with weeds to resemble the surrounding ground, and curtains of camouflage netting were hung over the front.

2nd Lieuts. Ainscough and Smith and the Right Section detachments did all the work in producing these roofed gun pits which happened to be the last of their kind ever made by the battery.

The social side of the battery life came into more prominence whilst at Metz than had hitherto been possible. Impromptu singsongs went on each night in the hutments, and led up to the idea of organising a battery concert. This took place on the 20th October. With some outside assistance quite a good programme was arranged. The piano had to be brought from Albert, and despite its long journey on wretched roads, had only some half-dozen notes out of action.

It was here also that the Battery Canteen first made its appearance, and did quite a thriving business. Cpl. Bennett was at this time in charge. We also had the advantage of other canteens within easy reach, including the E.F.C. at Ytres.

At the beginning of November we were first apprised of the possibility of this quiet part of the line becoming the scene of what turned out to be the most daring attack of the year. We did not then know how or where this attack was to take place, but the quiet preparations that were evidenced left little doubt that some offensive was projected.

On the 30th October, being so instructed, we moved the two Left Section guns from their position in Havrincourt Wood to a more advanced one on the left of that wood. This change, which was made by night, was not accomplished without great difficulty. The guns were hoisted on trucks on the Decauville Railway, which ran through the wood, and were hauled along by horses. So many obstacles presented themselves that, although operations were begun in the early evening, it was not until nearly 4 o'clock the following morning that the change was completed. This Section was now ordered to remain silent, except for S.O.S. calls.

The officers' mess was also considerably augmented by subalterns of various batteries being attached whilst in charge of digging operations preparatory to the coming attack. The prevailing thick, murky weather was undoubtedly favourable, in that in served to screen the industry that was everywhere being manifested. As a battery we were called on to arrange for the ammunition requirements of the incoming batteries, 2nd Lieut. G. A. Smith being given the direction of this work. An ammunition party of fifty of our number was kept busy dealing with huge consignments that came to the various parts of the Metz and Havrincourt Wood areas.

On the 15th November, many batteries moved silently into position, and others followed within the next two days. Scores of tanks were assembied by night, and concentrated in the woods ; and on the 17th November the redoubtable 51st (Highland) Division came to Metz and were billeted there.

Everything had been carried through with the greatest secrecy. Our own preparations were completed. The two guns from the Left Section after a period of inaction had been brought away and placed in position on the Gouzeaucourt Road, alongside the two already there, which had continued firing throughout these preparations.

At half-past five on the morning of the 18th November a small raid was made by the enemy, and there was some apprehension lest the impending attack had been discovered. This raid, however, was speedily repelled, and we were not called on to give assistance.

In addition to our preparations for the opening bombardment, all arrangements were made for the battery to move forward in anticipation of the attack being successful. Exact details were planned for this projected move. Owing to the time of year, and the consequent softened and broken condition of the roads, it was considered advisable to have horse haulage for the guns, and General Service wagons for the stores. The horses were found by the 119th Heavy Battery, who also found us a wagon lines officer. The wagons were packed with cookhouse requirements and rations for 70 men, gun stores, camouflage, stretchers, and medical stores, officers' and men's kits, signalling and B.C.A. stores. Water also had to be taken forward. All the first party were detailed to be in readiness. 38th Heavy Battery and ourselves were placed under the temporary control of 54th Group (Col. Dent), which was to act under the orders of the C.R.A. of the attacking division.

By the evening of the 19th November, having done all possible, we awaited the coming of the final despatches with such patience as could be mustered.

BOGGART'S HOLE (Oblique Air Photograph).

Showing "Boggart's Hole," where the trench mortar target was situated, and a large part of the ground over which the Battle of Cambrai was fought,

CHAPTER V.

THE BATTLE OF CAMBRAI.

The Battle of Cambrai differed wholly from any of our preceding offensives in that it depended largely for its success upon the element of surprise.

The objectives in view necessitated the smashing of the Hindenburg Main and Support Lines at their strongest points. Should these be successfully broken through the possibilities opened up were immense. The town of Cambrai lay beyond, and the high ground between offered the promise of great strategic advantage for any subsequent offensive. Great numbers of cavalry were massed behind us, and, on the day of the battle, covered the roads, to the great hindrance of the heavy artillery. What was to be the nature of their employment we do not, nor shall ever know. But there is no doubt that they performed many gallant actions.

Our target was a section of trench system containing strong points and machine-gun emplacements.

Zero hour on the 20th November was 6.20 a.m. Exactly to the second our guns opened out, and for three and a-half hours we continued firing, our ammunition expenditure in this time being 420 rounds.

The hazy morning gave assistance to the infantry and Tanks, who went over within four minutes of the opening of the barrage fire.

The surprise was complete; before we had finished our tasks, batches of prisoners were being brought back. Throughout the day this stream continued, and they bore unmistakable evidence of the strain they had been subjected to by our fire. News was eagerly sought, and we heard of successes at most points. There was a hold-up, however at the village of Flesquières, owing to the determined resistance of a comparatively small number of the enemy.

This delay had the effect of disarranging the time table to some extent, and affected ourselves in so far that we did not move forward as intended. We stood by the whole of the day ready to start should orders to do so arrive. Major Delap, accompanied by Mr. Bloye, went forward and carried out some reconnaissance work in the Havrincourt, Trescault, and Ribecourt areas, the results of which were furnished to Brigade Headquarters on their return. Tentative positions were also selected. That part of the battle which lay around Flesquières was clearly seen by them—several Tanks burning in front of the village, and others trying to outflank it under the fire of a German anti-tank gun. One battery of Horse Artillery had pushed up very close, and was endeavouring to silence the machine gunners concealed there. Without attempting to criticise the Higher Command, one may express regret for the silence of that great concentration of heavy artillery, all within range of Flesquières, who, if they had been allowed, could surely have made it untenable.

Night falling, it was definitely decided that we should not go forward that day. Later news came through that most objectives had been taken, and that several thousand prisoners and about 100 guns were in our hands. The battle position was satisfactory and prospects were favourable.

Our arrangements, with some minor modifications, remained the same, and when at last the importunities of the O.C. were acceded to, and instructions given for us to move forward, they were at once put in train.

An observation party, under 2nd Lieut. B. W. Yardley, accompanied by Bmdrs. Hancocks and Goldsmith and Signallers Dolphin and Pickles, went forward at 4.30 a.m. of the 21st. They established an O.P., but its usefulness was largely nullified by the fast-moving battle. They remained on duty, however, until the following day, when they rejoined the battery.

A small advance party, under the leadership of 2nd Lieut. Bloye, was the next to leave, taking with them selected stores, and by 10 o'clock the guns and the whole of the personnel detailed to go forward were on the move.

During the second day of the battle, successes unforeseen fell to our divisions. These successes necessitated changes in our plans, and being made while on the move, slightly dislocated the working of the arrangements, the party principally affected being the advance party, who failed to make contact again with the main body until late that night.

After some halts en route our guns were pulled into position at Trescault, and the line of fire laid out in the early failing light. It was not a cheery time. The weather was raw and foggy, and the knowledge that success had been added to success failed to give warmth to the personnel. When, however, the cooks had arranged to prepare some tea, a higher tone pervaded us, and such shelter as the ruins afforded was sought for the night.

We were unable to take any part in the battle. The line had been advanced from the Flesquières Ridge, and the end of the second day found our infantry at the foot of the high ground of Bourlon Hill and Wood. The roads had, however, been badly blown up, and great craters lay between ourselves and the advanced line, making it impossible for us to go forward. The uncertainty of our front also made it impossible for us to fire from where we were. We were, however, prepared to take part, if called on, the guns being laid on the S.O.S. lines that were furnished.

The third day of the battle was passed in this same position, and advantage was taken of the lull to bring forward further supplies of ammunition and stores, which were unloaded and later served as a forward dump for the battery.

We were attached temporarily to the 51st Divisional Artillery. We were ready and anxious to go forward, and could now have done so if we had been allowed. The disadvantage of attachment to Divisional Artillery in a battle of this kind was here apparent, for notwithstanding the great effect upon the operations which the introduction of a 6″ battery might have produced, the Divisional Artillery were unwilling to order us forward for fear of blocking the road.

A new advance was now begun in the hope of consolidating our gains by securing possession of the important strategic points of Bourlon and Fontaine.

In support of these operations, we received orders on the night of 22nd November to move forward the following morning. We accordingly paraded at 4.30 a.m. There were some absentees, but all were shortly acounted for, with the exception of Cpl. Sharp, who was the n.c.o. in charge of the signallers. An exhaustive search was made for him but with no avail until the breaking dawn, when, as the result of careful observation we were led to the conclusion that he had fallen down a partially hidden but uncovered well. Everything possible was done, but without immediate success. The recovery of his body later proved, unhappily, that our suspicions were correct. Cpl. Sharp was an exceedingly conscientious and popular n.c.o., and his death threw a gloom over all as we moved out without him.

Passing through the village of Ribecourt, we pulled into positon on the Flesquières Ridge, in the same vicinity where the Tanks had suffered so severely earlier in the battle. Immediately to our rear stood what was left of the house we had previously used as a datum point for registering and calibrating our guns. To bring our guns into position we had to haul them up a steep bank, which proved an almost insuperable task. And before this was finally achieved, we had hastily to construct a roadway. In doing this we utilised the bricks from the "datum" house that we had helped to destroy.

The C.R.A. 51st Division himself welcomed us to our new position, and gave us as our first target Fontaine village, which it was intended shortly to attack.

We were in the midst of the Hindenburg Line, and the support trench which passed on our right flank provided temporary cover. Immediate registration for line was obtained from a point in Fontaine village—a derelict Tank on the crest making an excellent observation post.

Other targets were sent through to us coming direct from the Division, in support of whom we were operating.

We constructed temporary shelters in the support trench near to the position, and further search discovered an exceedingly elaborate system of dug-outs, which had been the headquarters of a German F.A. Brigade. These were taken over as our own headquarters the next day, and also provided billets for the detachments off duty.

The first night, however, was spent in the trenches, and it turned out to be a very wet and tempestuous one. Tents were pitched and used by the officers, but went down before the storm during the night. The trench became waterlogged, and having a chalk substratum covered our stores and persons with a mortar-like mixture. The morning dawned at last, a bright sunshine and crisp air succeeding the storm.

Our guns were kept busy firing on target after target as the fluctuating fortunes of the attack demanded. The roads from Cambrai were specially searched by our fire. Calls were answered from any direction in which it was possible for us to switch. Targets in

Bourlon were followed by others in Fontaine and the districts south of Cambrai.

After being accustomed to firing from carefully concealed gun positions it was a change to us to find ourselves on an open hillside, amidst all the movement of a battle, Tanks in front, cavalry behind, and the road packed with every kind of traffic.

During this day and those that followed the detachments worked manfully under Sergts. Redrup, Tanner, Turner, Parnell, Coe, and Nicholls, hampered as they were by the mud and rain and snow.

Considerable difficulty was experienced in getting rations. Biscuits and bully beef were the staple diet, when obtainable, although expectation had on occasion to serve as substitute. But it was a time of good comradeship, and some unofficial liaisons were established with the infantry.

Some very interesting finds were made in the dug-outs we took possession of. Amongst others we discovered a German artillery map with our various positions marked. Included in these, our first Right Section position near Havrincourt Wood was correctly shown, together with the date of the destructive shoot they had carried out on us.

We were constantly subject to enemy fire, especially at night, and this increased in intensity as the days passed. Our casualties were very light, Gnr. McManus being wounded on the 26th, and Gnr. Stevenson on the 27th. Both of these went to hospital. There were, however, several very narrow escapes, and the guns sustained damage, but not sufficient to put them out of action.

The repeated efforts that were being made to obtain possession of Bourlon and the high ground beyond Fontaine proved unavailing. The Guards Division suffered heavily at Fontaine, and the 62nd Division, who had fought so gallantly, failed to hold what they had won in Bourlon. The Germans had been by now tremendously reinforced, and on the 30th November they made a determined effort to close the salient formed by our advance.

Our impressions of the 30th November will always be very vivid. The view from the O.P. was obscured by smoke, so that we could not see the movements of any of the enemy infantry, but we knew that he was attempting something serious on our front by the calls for S.O.S. barrage fire received. As the morning went on his shell fire on the battery areas increased, and we received orders to fire on many different targets. At about 9.30 a.m. one of the guns that had been annoying us became so persistent that the detachment of No. 1 gun was ordered away, the rate of fire being maintained with the other guns. At this time a great deal of movement in our neighbourhood warned us that all was not well. About thirty Tanks which had been standing near trundled off to the right, one of them being hit just after it had started. Field batteries were galloping about taking up new positions and pointing in new directions. Lines of infantry could be seen in extended order crossing the country to our right and behind us. The village of Ribecourt, which lay immediately behind us, was all this time being heavily shelled. It may be added that our telephone line to Brigade was so constantly cut by shell fire that it was impossible to keep it going, and communication was kept up by runner instead.

At about 10.30 one of the runners (Signaller Warner) arrived with the order: "Stand by to destroy your guns," and this was accordingly done, long lanyards of telephone wire being laid into a convenient trench, and 106 fuses being prepared for the removal of their tapes

We then received a series of conflicting orders arising from the confusion of the situation and the fact that the Brigade Commander and the Adjutant were in different places, each doing his best, but out of touch with one another. We were to "pull out all guns at once," "Leave two guns in action and pull out the other two," "Four teams are coming to pull you out," and so on.

At last one team arrived, and we were instructed to send one gun away to Havrincourt and get the other three away as best we could to the light railway behind Ribecourt, over half-a-mile away, and take them away by train to Bus, if possible. The team was used to pull each gun out of its position on to the road; one gun was sent away to Havrincourt with Lieut. Smith and a party, and the other three were dragged by sheer man power through the village to the railway, only to find another battery there with its guns astride the rail, ready for the train, which had not come.

All this weary afternoon the road had swarmed with a crowd of guns, limbers, wagons, horses, lorries—all those fortunate units which had means of transport at their disposal. Mingled with these had been many wounded hobbling back to dressing stations at Trescault, and a large number of gas casualties from a gas concentration out Marcoing way.

Eventually the train arrived, and the battery that was waiting for it was soon packed on the special gun trucks. Just as they were leaving, which they did with many condolences and promising to send the train back when they had finished with it, an officer from the Guards Division Artillery came up and said they thought the situation had eased a bit, and asked us to get into action forthwith, and go on shelling Fontaine.

By this time the road had cleared—all that hurrying traffic had gone, even the Field Artillery were no more to be seen, though they were actually getting into position a good way behind us. Enemy shells still fell in Ribecourt and all that valley, and a complete state of uncertainty as to the whereabouts of the enemy existed, in our minds at least.

By half-past eight the guns had been pulled into their new position on platforms left by 68th Siege Battery, the "line" laid out, fire on the village of Fontaine resumed, and a message sent to the "Guards D.A." that the battery was again in action.

There was now some opportunity of seeking shelter and getting food and cover. The only cover we could find was the arch of the bridge where the main road crosses an insignificant ditch known as "Grand Ravine." This was immediately adopted by the cooks, signallers, and anyone who wanted to get out of the rain, and it was not until we had five men wounded there that we discovered that the enemy was trying to knock it down.

CHAPTER VI.

RIBECOURT.

Within the next few days our line became more stabilised, although there were still many critical times. It was decided, however, that we should continue to hold the position that we had hastily taken up; and there we stayed until March, though two guns were moved to a rear position as described. It was a strange site for a 6″ battery, being 1,100 yards from the front line: we often suffered from bursts of hostile machine-gun bullets, and our "S.O.S." was 1st charge 10°, which "speaks volumes." The days succeeding were fully occupied in building shelters along the ravine, in firing on hostile attacks, and in dodging the shells that were constantly being showered on us.

Telephonic communication was maintained with difficulty—although on one occasion, early in December, we were the only heavy artillery that could be called. The need was pressing. A hostile attack was being massed on the south side of Nine Wood, and in response to an urgent call we opened fire almost instantly. First charge only was required as the range was barely 1,200 yards. So effective was the result that the impending attack was completely broken up.

While we were in this position the organisation of the Heavy Artillery was altered by the substitution of the Brigade for the Group system. Batteries thenceforward were brigaded permanently under one Brigade instead of being attached only temporarily to a Group; 29th H.A.G. became the 29th (Mobile) Brigade, R.G.A., consisting of 12th H.B., 121st H.B., 195th S.B., and 303rd S.B. Here also Lieut.-Col. Macalpine-Leny, D.S.O., left Brigade on being invalided to England, and was replaced by Lieut.-Col. A. D. Murray, D.S.O. On his first visit to the Battery Lieut. Ledward showed something less than his usual perspicacity in mistaking the latter for "the new Padre"!

Our position here was a very precarious one. The support trenches were behind us. We were instructed, however, to hold on, although later it was deemed advisable to move two of the guns to another position almost midway between Ribecourt and Trescault. This was carried into effect on the 11th December, our No. 1 and No. 3 guns being selected.

This new position we were to take up and which became known as the Rear Position, was about as unpromising as could well be imagined. It was absolutely devoid of natural cover. The site had formerly been used as horse lines whilst the Germans held it.

The two guns were placed in position in a slight hollow and camouflaged. The provision of shelter for the gun detachments and of a command post was not so easily arranged. It was decided, however, to construct dug-out accommodation for the season by digging from the surface to a depth of 10 feet, and forming chambers by means of elephant iron sections resting on supports, and then filling in again above with the displaced earth. This scheme naturally occupied much time before completion, and meanwhile such cover had to be taken advantage of as was afforded by the pits whilst under construction.

Billets were also found at Trescault and absorbed a lot of labour in making them reasonably proof against hostile shelling. These billets were primarily intended for the use of the Rear Section detachments off duty, but they later came to be used generally by both sections, and, at a later time still, became the rear Headquarters of the battery.

Very shortly after the formation of the Rear Section it was subjected to enemy shelling. In fact the first night was marked by a casualty, Gnr. Joynson being hit by a shell splinter and taken to hospital. A couple of nights later Gnr. Mitchell was more seriously wounded during a short area strafe. Considerable difficulty was necessarily experienced in attending to his injuries and his subsequent removal to hospital. Cpl. Potter with six gunners successfully undertook this duty.

Meanwhile events at the Forward Position were happening worthy of recollection. One of the most interesting of these was the salving of a German 5·9 naval gun, which had been abandoned on the 20th November. A party was detailed from the battery under Capt. Bennett, Sergt.-Major Steel, and Sergt. Nicholls, the O.C. also accompanying them. The work was undertaken at night, and despite the great weight of the gun, the party skilfully handled it to the road, where it was handed over and taken away by tractor. This incident has since formed the subject of a picture illustrative of artillery work.

The water supply at this position was temporarily interfered with, the well head having a direct hit. The officers' quarters also suffered damage on another occasion. In fact, the whole appearance of the district became changed with the constant shelling.

The need for dug-out accomodation being early realised, work was soon begun on a most commodious one, with double entrance, sunk to a depth of 18 feet. The making of this kept us busy, in fact, the many projects that were being carried out tested the capabilities of the battery to the utmost. At a later time we had the assistance of an Australian Tunnelling Company. Difficulties were experienced in obtaining supplies of R.E. material, and when obtained, transport shortage, and the broken state of the roads presented further problems.

The Christmas season was now fast approaching, and there was, in spite of our not enlivening surroundings, an air of expectancy. What, indeed, was hoped for it is difficult to record. Some boldly foresaw the cessation of hostilities, while others rumoured a change in position. Neither of these hopes was to be realised.

Winter set in in real earnest, and for some three weeks heavy snowstorms succeeded one another, and thickly covered the ground. This considerably interfered with our digging operations, and other methods of camouflage had to be devised. Calico sheets were employed to cover the guns and blast marks. The shell holes were filled up with the snow, and proved a constant source of surprise to wary and unwary alike.

At this time our numbers were being much reduced by an outbreak of trench fever, aggravated no doubt by the arduous conditions.

We carried out some quite successful shoots during December. Occupying, as we did, so unusually advanced positions, our targets were largely counter-battery, and we were fully called on for such work with both aeroplane and ground observation. We were in close touch with the infantry, and had co-operation with the Field Survey and Balloon Companies.

Christmas Eve was not without its excitements. At 3 o'clock in the morning Ribecourt and district were subjected to an intense and prolonged gas bombardment. The front line, too, was being heavily shelled, and responding to their calls we fired on our S.O.S. lines. Communication being cut between the sections, runners had to be employed, Gnrs. Fish and Hawtin being detailed for this work. We had the good fortune to come through this trying time without casualty.

Christmas Day passed very quietly for both sections. In the forenoon there was some desultory shelling, and we sent over a few rounds in response. Otherwise the day was given over to such festivities as could be mustered. With a little plum pudding, two nuts, and an apple, an imaginative man can work up a Christmassy feeling anywhere.

This short lull was rudely broken in upon before the dawn on Boxing Day. Again we were subjected to an area bombardment, both gas and H.E. being used, and again we escaped without casualty, but we were called on to render such assistance as we could to neighbouring Field Batteries who had fared less fortunately. Later in the day, after the bombardment had ceased, Gnr. Whitehouse was instantly killed by a shell whilst working on the position at the Forward Section.

The few remaining days of the Old Year were chiefly notable for constant shelling, great activity being manifested by the enemy, culminating in an attack on Welsh Ridge which lay on our right flank.

After the Battle of Cambrai our attitude was changed from an offensive to a purely defensive one. The enemy policy was less quiescent, and on the 30th December they made a determined attempt to take Welsh Ridge. We shared in the opening bombardment and suffered two casualties, Sig. Matheson being killed, and Sig. Warner seriously wounded by a shell bursting in the shelter which they occupied. The attack was successfully held after a severe struggle, in which we took an active part.

This attack was accompanied by a heavy bombardment on the battery areas, suspected positions receiving special attention. S.O.S. being called for, the two guns of the Forward Section (the Nos. 1 being Sergts. Coe and Stead, and Lieut. Johnson the officer on duty) maintained their rate of fire under very heavy neutralisation. The

(Air Photographs).

25.1.18   **GERMAN BATTERY No. LX7.**   16.2.18

Photographs taken before and after a shoot by *one gun* of 303 Siege Battery Forward Section at Ribecourt.

(Observed by 15 Squadron, R.F.C.).

rear section was also engaged as heavily as the forward section, 5'9 gas and H.E. being used. In the absence of any orders, the telephone lines having gone, Capt. Bennett and Lieut. Bloye, acting on information received from a neighbouring Field Battery, opened on their S.O.S. lines. The detachment of the No. 1 gun were obliged to work in their respirators. The personnel on duty in both sections deserve great credit for the determination shown.

This hostile activity was maintained, and the New Year had barely been ushered in before we were being heavily shelled. Within the first few minutes of 1918 we had three casualties at the Rear Position; Gnr. Purdy was gassed and Gnrs. Beveridge and Fish wounded, the latter so severely that he shortly afterwards died of his wounds.

Early in the New Year we received many reinforcements to replace those who had gone; but some of these were unable to stand the arduous life, and very speedily were compelled to report sick and were sent to hospital. Lieut. S. Johnson had also joined the battery on the 20th December.

The outstanding features of this winter warfare were the bursts of fire to which we were subjected and the close observation maintained by enemy planes. This observation necessitated constant precautions and interfered materially with our carrying out prolonged shoots. Despite this watchfulness, however, we did a great amount of damage to enemy battery positions.

On the 25th January, during one of these bursts of fire, we suffered loss by the death of 2nd Lieut. T. A. Ainscough and B.S.M. Steel. They had both very recently returned from leave, and had barely got into the swing of battery life again when this unhappy disaster occurred. One of the guns was also badly damaged and had to be sent away, leaving only a single gun at the Forward Section. This one gun, however, did some very successful work, and on the 26th January one of our most notable shoots was carried out with it. On the previous day we had been having a destructive shoot on an enemy position, and after the gun had got well ranged and done considerable damage, the airman who was observing for us noticed another battery near by that was showing great activity. He at once switched us off our target to this new one, the range being found almost immediately. Darkness, however, prevented us from continuing, but the following day we were given an allotment of ammunition and ordered to continue the shoot. This was quite successful, and was considered to be so good an example of a destructive shoot, and of the co-operation between aircraft and artillery, that the photographs taken by the airman showing the German battery positions both before and after our shoot, were used as an example by 15th Squadron, R.A.F.

Our rations during these winter months were good, although there was great difficulty at times in getting them forward to the positions. The road between Trescault and Ribecourt was a special target for enemy batteries, and on occasion hours would be occupied in trying to get the wagon safely through. The state of the roads necessitated the use of general service wagons, our own transport

3.

being found other employment. The drivers had many hairbreadth escapes, and though this road was the scene of many disasters, our service was maintained without loss.

The dispatch riders and runners, too, had no easy task, and Gnr. Fletcher, who has held the post of dispatch rider throughout the period of active service, lived a distinctly adventurous life. He was assisted at this time by Gnrs. Fryer and Jones, the aeroplane spotters.

The hopes that had been tenaciously clung to throughout, that we were to have a change in position or to go out on rest, now gave a promise of realisation.

The Higher Command were preparing to withstand the shocks of an anticipated spring offensive. Units were in turn being withdrawn from the line and given a period of rest, combined with training for defensive warfare. And it now became definitely understood that we were to share in this scheme, and that the end of February would probably be the limit of our stay in the Ribecourt and Trescault areas, if, indeed, it had not been terminated already by the offensive for which the enemy was known to be preparing.

In anticipation of such a contingency we had to make dispositions best calculated to hold up an advance. The elevations required for short range firing for each gun were calculated and various other preparations made. As circumstances turned out, the threatened offensive was delayed until after our departure.

CHAPTER VII.

AT REST.

When the time came for leaving this unhealthy salient we all breathed a sigh of relief. Looking back to those days we can feel proud that we held a forward position for so long, and by doing so reached Hun batteries that no one else could touch; but it must be admitted that the constant strain of the shelling, and the knowledge that but one line of trenches protected our guns from capture, had told upon us very much.

As the time for the departure of the Forward Section from Ribecourt drew near, the enemy's attentions most mysteriously increased; so much so that one wondered whether he had somehow "tumbled to it" that we were pulling out. He kept a 4·2 gun sending a "time H.E." shell dead over the position at half-minute intervals; while every twenty minutes he poured in a very rapid concentration of 4·2″ and 77mm. ground bursts. There was nothing for it but to ignore the half-minute time shell, and dodge for cover during the concentrations. Fortunately the "line" of these latter was about fifty yards out, and remained there; but a strafe of forty shells a minute when you are doing difficult work in the dark is disturbing, to say the least of it.

By the irony of fate we were to be relieved by a section of 68th Siege Battery, who had given place to us on the 30th November. They had left us with condolences on our position, and we could do no less than return these on their reappearance. This relieving section turned up at 11 p.m. during a quiet interval, and by this time, as our guns and stores were ready loaded on the Decauville train, we wasted no time in getting them away with their detachments. They eventually arrived safely at Etricourt, after having to man the drag ropes to pull the loaded train up a slope, which was beyond the power of the engine. Meanwhile those left behind completed the formalities of handing over and departed on foot to Trescault, with no regrets and probably thankful hearts.

The Rear Section was to move on the following night, the 26th, and though they also were shelled while the Forward Section was pulling out, it did not matter so much as they were able to take cover.

The removal from the Rear Position was carried through under easier conditions. After a short concentration in the afternoon, we were left alone. We were ready for the train at 5 p.m., everything being in order alongside the Decauville. We had repaired the line, badly cut by shell fire in our vicinity, and the short siding by which ammunition was brought up was lined with guns and stores. There was no sign of the train—we learned later that much repair had been necessary further down the line—so we lit our station lamp (a candle in a wooden box) and sat or lay cramped in the dug-outs or on the steps of the sap. Our numbers were increased by the party from billets, and our accommodation was tried to the utmost.

The trucks, which were due at 7 p.m., did not arrive till 1 a.m. (27th). The welcome news of "train up" wakened us, and willing hands soon put the guns and all stores abroad. At this point a difficulty arose. The engine pulled the trucks, with guns, stores, and personnel down the slope to the main line easily enough, but could not drag them up the hill. So the trucks with the men were left behind till the engine had pulled the guns and stores up on to the level ground. What our thoughts were as we waited for the engine to return is more easily remembered than written. A few wrapped themselves up and tried to sleep in the cold morning air, but the majority of us walked about in some trepidation lest further shelling should interfere with our departure. After an hour of suspense the engine returned, and soon the position was lost to sight, though not to memory. Our relief on quitting the position was real and heartfelt. Surely we never could find a hotter corner than the famous Cambrai salient.

We left a guard of six men, under Bmdr. McGill, at Trescault billets and the Trescault position. Shelling of the billets, which had been intermittent before we left, continued much the same. On 2nd March shells fell uncomfortably close, and those within decided to seek safer shelter elsewhere and started out. Bmdr. McGill was wounded by splinters and went to hospital and home.

While we were leaving Trescault the Right Section reached Etricourt and got under canvas (3 a.m.), and here we joined them at about 8 a.m. At mid-day all marched to entrain for the promised rest. We travelled for four hours over the famous Somme battlefield, where, however, the trenches were already covered with vegetation, and only blasted trees and those saddening enclosures of little wooden crosses seemed to mark the struggle that had been waged in 1916. Here and there were salvage dumps on which gangs of Allied colonials of variegated colour showed their white teeth as they smiled at us. At 5.15 p.m. we reached Buire and got tea from the canteen on the platform. We were once again among French peasants; and to many of us the sight of civilians was welcome—we had seen only soldiers for a long time.

From Buire we marched to the pleasant little village of Ville-sous-Corbie, or Ville-sur-Ancre, for it boasted of both names. Here we were billeted in the large "granges" or barns of a farm. We had beds, too. True, they were merely wire-netting on a wooden framework, but after wet ground or hard boards they seemed luxurious.

While we travelled by train Lieuts. Ledward and Oliver were bringing the guns by road. That party spent the night of the 27th in Bapaume, where Capt. Bennett, who had just returned from leave, joined it, and it was further augmented by Lieut. Green, who, with Sergt. Nicholls, had just returned from Calais with the two new guns to complete our establishment. Thus, when this party reached Ville-sous-Corbie about mid-day the battery was once again at full strength. That evening we parked the guns on the soft ground between the billets and the church, and proceeded to make ourselves at home in the cafés. All anticipated a few weeks of comparatively idle ease, and we were determined to enjoy them.

Fate willed it otherwise. We had been withdrawn for rest, but also to be in support, should the great German offensive develop. After a very few days of this life, idyllic compared with that of the preceding months, we received orders to move up, where we could be more readily called upon at short notice. Away from all signs of war we thought the Army had "the wind up," and that we were being badly treated. Everyone knows the first duty of a soldier, and when, following instructions that reached us at 11.30 p.m. on the snowy evening of 2nd March, we were ordered to advance on 3rd March, we re-packed our stores, limbered up the guns, and got smartly on the way. Along the highway through Albert, with its sadly demolished church and houses, we re-traversed the Somme battle ground and swung through Bapaume to Beaulencourt. There we were allotted a number of Nissen huts and occupied them by subsections, and there the remainder of our rest was spent.

We set to work to improve the conditions of our camp. We made roads, built huts, and dug them partly in, sorted stores, etc. For the making of roads we obtained permission to cart bricks from Le Transloy, where what were once houses were now mere heaps of bricks. We helped our sister batteries to build roads, too, and to prepare "standings" for their horses.

That was the morning's work. After tea we were free to visit Bapaume, a town that was in ruins, where even the cellars had been reached by shell or bomb. Bapaume was the rail-head for men going on leave, and the increasing allotment did even more than the rest to cheer us up. We were out of the war, yet in it, for we could hear the boom of the artillery and watch the night flares as we noted the flashes of the heavy guns. In Bapaume there were many attractions. Canteens, wet and dry, catered fully for our needs and fancies; in the Theatre the "Tonics" ran an amusing and most attractive revue, entitled "Some Dodger" every night except Saturday, when it became a picture house. There were also baths (a great luxury), and the officers had a club, which they are said to have enjoyed, notwithstanding the draughts and the rats.

But perhaps the most enjoyable day of all was that on which we holidayed in Amiens. We left camp early in the morning, and travelling by lorry to Achiet-le-Grand, proceeded by train to the Cathedral City. The weather was well-nigh perfect, and we wandered at our own sweet wills through the city, charmed with the perfection of the Gothic cathedral, the allurements of shop windows, the attractions of cafés, and so forth. We came back in good humour in the evening to send home souvenirs of the city of the Somme.

Sports were fostered round the camp in the afternoons, and even shell holes on the football fields did not spoil many keen games. We had many fine players in the battery, and could select a strong representative eleven to meet other teams. Perhaps the most interesting afternoon was that on which we carried through an inter-section competition, organised by Mr. Smith, from which the Signallers emerged worthy winners, defeating "C" sub. narrowly in the final. We fared unevenly with other battery teams, winning on some occasions, on others suffering defeat, but always returning satisfied with the game. We watched, too, occasional bouts with the gloves, but no tournament was held.

During our rest a layer's class was formed, the opening lecture being delivered by the O.C. The other officers carried on the practical work in turn, and just before we pulled back into action every member of the class was familiar with the dial sight and the duties of a layer.

We knew that we had been moved to Beaulencourt in accordance with military requirements, but to us there was little indication of a pending attack. The O.C. spent several days in examining the area we were likely to occupy in such a contingency to find support positions, and on the following days the other officers also reconnoitred this part. All this was, of course, absolutely necessary work, but we scarcely realised its full significance.

The Army summer began during out rest, and on the morning of Sunday, 10th March, we found ourselves out of bed an hour earlier than usual, and yet at the customary time. A week later (17th March) the Colonel inspected the personnel of the four batteries drawn up in quarter column in front of 121st Heavy Battery's Horse Lines. This inspection was followed by divine service in the open.

We shall always think gratefully of this time of rest, the only rest we had except for a day or two between positions. The hopes that we had entertained of a real rest came to naught, and it was a great disappointment being moved from Ville-sur-Ancre. In spite of the time taken up in fatigues, we were able to do some training of a necessary kind, and we could hardly have carried on without it. The building that we did of huts and horse lines was mostly waste, for it all fell into the hands of the Hun before it was finished; but it is possible that the huts survived, and were used by our troops when the enemy was driven back.

No sense of impending catastrophe was felt by us, though we were on the brink of the great retreat, and our armies were about to face the hardest fighting of the war.

CHAPTER VIII.
THE GREAT GERMAN OFFENSIVE.

For months we had been expecting a German attack. The collapse of Russia had released huge numbers of German troops from the Eastern front.

The German High Command, for all that they belittled the American preparations, must have known that America was coming to the assistance of the Allies in increasing strength, and that before long the numerical superiority which they had gained would be counterbalanced.

This reasoning, even more than the preparations for attack which our airmen had been able to detect, warned the Allied Command to prepare to withstand a great onslaught. On all sides one heard confident predictions as to the date of the great offensive, and at 4 a.m. on 21st March we realised that the moment had arrived.

The walls and windows in the huts of our Beaulencourt Rest Camp were set rattling by a mighty roar bursting from every part of the line. The weight and persistence of this bombardment put it beyond all doubt that the long expected attack had materialised. Every gun that the Hun could boast must have been hard at work. Even Bapaume, which at that time was far behind our lines, was under fire from his long-range guns.

Immediately preparations were made for an early start; the stores were packed, guns limbered up, and by 9 a.m. we were all ready for the road. Orders meanwhile had been received from Brigade that we were to reconnoitre positions in the Fremicourt area, and remain under half-an-hour's notice to move. It had not yet been decided whether the Brigade was to go into action at once or to be held in reserve.

We moved forward towards dusk, and benefitting by a fair moon just in its first quarter, passed through the villages of Bancourt and Fremicourt. Just beyond the latter village the F.W.D.'s pulled up on the roadside short of the railway, and from there the guns were man-hauled into position behind the railway embankment. One after another they were got into action, platforms being made from the heavy planking that buttressed the wooden huts close under the bank. In the darkness we opened fire, endeavouring to help stay the enemy, whose rapid progress was such as to admit of no delay in our participation. Firing continued steadily, and an odd hour's sleep was all that we could snatch. Throughout the next day we fired without intermission, target succeeding target in bewildering succession, so that it was difficult to open fire on one before an order to cease and open fire on another came over the 'phone. The range was shortening steadily and rapidly—charge 4 gave place to charges 3 and 2—it was evident that, despite our constant efforts, the advance was scarcely being stayed. On the other hand our airmen sent us the reassuring and heartening report that we were inflicting terrible casualties on the advancing hordes. Before us lay the glorious 51st (Highland) Division, composed of Scottish Territorials. Had the dogged resistance which they offered been maintained in other sectors, the Hun offensive would never have succeeded. By early evening the railway track was the support line, and we fraternised with those fine soldiers. We were being shelled, too, but our only casualty was from a premature on a 60-pounder behind us, when Wheeler-Gunner W. L. Nixon was wounded, and Lieut. Green's breeches torn.

The Major has memories of disquieting rumours that reached us that day. In the morning we were told on most reliable authority that the Huns were in Beugny and coming on fast, and anxious conferences took place between the Battery Commanders as to how many men could be spared to line the railway with rifles. An O.P. out on the hill in front was manned for a time by the Major and Mr. Bloye, whence swarms of the enemy could be seen pouring over the shell-spattered slopes.

In the evening we pulled back through Bancourt to the outskirts of Bapaume, where once more we found billets in wooden huts.

The first position was already being swept by machine-gun fire when the guns left. On the battery's arrival at the next position Mr. Oliver volunteered to take charge of a party in lorries to fetch the ammunition remaining, and this was successfully done without casualty.

We were unable to keep an accurate account of the ammunition we were expending, and here, at Bancourt Road, we made use of a supply that had just been brought up by rail.

The Colonel, who visited the batteries several times during the day, told us a story that heartened us very much. One target, which the whole brigade was ordered to engage, was a concentration of the enemy, massing for an attack, in full view of our infantry. Gun fire from all four batteries fell amongst them, inflicting terrible casualties. Just then they started to advance, still in mass formation, and at the same moment Corps H.A., who had been asked by the infantry to engage the target, ordered a drop in range of 500 yards. This was pure chance or Providence; but the result was that the attacking force, coming for a second time under the fire of the brigade, simply melted away. We had thus one German attack stopped, entirely to the credit of the brigade, without infantry action.

Enemy fire was directed on Bapaume and the Beaulencourt Road, and several short shots fell around and among us, driving those off duty to seek shelter in old shell holes and behind mounds. Fortunately no damage was reported. All the next day, although we had orders to stand by to move at 9 a.m., we carried on the work, loosing a continuous succession of shells on the still progressing enemy, whose good fortune in the matter of weather was still proverbial. On the afternoon following we were ordered to pull out. Bapaume was now clear of our men, and the canteens were already busy hives of "scroungers," who tried to prevent anything from falling into German hands. Nor, if one may judge by the ample supplies of cigarettes, tobacco, chocolate, biscuits, and even drink, that were freely handled or hawked about, were they unsuccessful!

We must have been the last heavy battery to pull out through deserted Bapaume. We watched the shells bursting among its ruins and on its streets. Two of the guns lost their girdles in the passage through the town, but a party was sent back and salved them.

We had to run the gauntlet of a particularly unpleasant 5·9 gun, which was shelling the corner leading into Bapaume with great accuracy. Taking a loaded column past that point was nasty work, but to our surprise all the vehicles passed it in safety.

We pulled in at Thilloy, alongside an excellent camp of wooden huts that had just been hurriedly evacuated by the R.E.'s. Stores of many kinds had been left behind, and we secured many "trophies." We fitted ourselves with brand-new leather jerkins; the Signallers secured a gramophone with its selection of records, and had space been available, we should have carried away a fine piano! Here, then, after getting the guns into action, we chose billets for ourselves, and here tea was got ready. But just as the cooks were issuing our tea ration, orders came through for another move.

The guns were man-handled with considerable difficulty over the rough ground to the F.W.D.'s on the road, and we moved back still further. We learned later that our hurried movements were not without cause; that another half-hour would have made us prisoners at the best, and our guns Hun trophies of war!

We moved back through Grevillers, where Lieut. Green, taking a wrong turning with two of the guns, was running hard into the enemy's arms when he found his mistake. We got off the F.W.D.'s, turned the guns a second time, and overtook the others without incident. Half-way between Grevillers and Irles, at Loupart Wood, where the infantry were already digging in, we pulled into action along a by-road. Orders were given to prepare a C.P. in a lorry, but before anything could be done we were on the move again.

At this point things were going badly for our retreat. The Brigade had been allotted certain roads for retirement, roads almost unfit for heavy artillery. Five minutes' rain would have made them impassable for us. The darkness and the great crowds made it difficult to keep communication with our headquarters, and this was absolutely vital. By a combination of luck and strict obedience to instructions, all the Battery Commanders were able to make contact with the Colonel at Bihucourt, and get their orders for the next move. So close a thing was it that a puncture to the tyres of the car would probably have brought about the capture of the battery.

It was now dark, and the long line of transport would have made an excellent target for an enterprising airman. We remained a long time at Irles, and were forced to wait again owing to the steep descent at the entrance to Miraumont, where the road crosses the Ancre river. Here we turned north and spent the night on the road leading to Achiet-le-Petit, reaching the village soon after dawn on 25th March. We received orders to get into action at Serre, a place we got to know better later, at least by name. It seemed as if our retreat were over, and we proceeded through Puisieux to Serre. In the ruined village we met the General and Colonel, who gave us orders to push on. Our retreat was not over yet. Our route took us over ground with which we all became very familiar in the next phase of our history. Past Colincamp's Sugary, by Mailly-Maillet,

Beaussart, and Bertrancourt, we went to Acheux, where we stopped to billet for the night. We took advantage of the break to have a wash in the horse pond at the entrance to the village, but here we were not destined to remain. Orders were received to billet at Marieux on the main road to Doullens. We arrived there about 11.30 p.m. to find that all available billets were occupied. There was nothing for it but to push on to Sarton, where we were more fortunate, for we found a sleeping-place in a comfortable barn, and lay down at about 1 a.m. to get what sleep we could.

Next morning we were able to post field cards and green envelope letters in the Area Commandant's office, and felt relieved to think that those at home would soon know we were safe, despite the conflicting news of the day.

Only those who saw can realise the scenes of that great retreat, the greatest retreat in point of numbers, if not of distance, which has ever taken place: the crowded miles of traffic on every road and track, the difficulties from inevitable breakdowns, the continual disorganisation caused by the rapid movements, the wounded trailing to the dressing station only to find that it had moved, the glare from burning camps destroyed to deny them to the enemy, the aeroplanes wheeling overhead and signalling us on—who will ever forget the cold and fatigue and the bitter disappointment of having to retreat. It must not be forgotten that when a battery moves, whether by day or night, the road must first be reconnoitred and the next battery position found, rations must be got by hook or by crook, and petrol for twenty-one great vehicles. All this was done and it was no light task, through days and nights and unfamiliar roads and the great crowds of hurrying armies.

Next day the orders were to move on, and billet somewhere in the neighbourhood of Frohen-le-Grand. We passed through Doullens, where there was some excitement. A conference of Allied Generals was evidently about to take place. Field-Marshall Sir Douglas Haig was seen on the steps of the Mairie, and several French Generals were arriving in motor-cars. Here, fortunately, we were able to get rations. Our larder was quite empty, and here also we heard and tried to ignore many disquieting rumours. One which we heard was to the effect that German armoured cars had crossed our lines at Arras, and were even then making for Doullens, and the O.C. heard arrangements being made for our Motor Machine Gunners to go and meet them. We went on through Mezerolles and Frohen-le-Grand, which was crowded with batteries, so we turned up to Le Meillard and billetted ourselves there for the night of 26th March.

New orders reached us, that only horse-drawn batteries would remain in the line, and thus our tractor-drawn guns were to remain out of action meantime, and we were for a few days taken off the strength of the 29th Brigade.

Our guns had been left under a guard on the main road east of Frohen-le-Grand, and we were ordered to remain near them. It was necessary, therefore, to erect tents for the men, and in these or in "bivvies" and a barn we spent the night after marching down the hill. Though we did not realise it at the moment, our retreat was finished: we had made our first move back into the arena.

CHAPTER IX.
BEAUSSART.

That afternoon (28th March) saw us once more moving back to the realities of war. A party of 30 went on to load ammunition from the dump at the railhead at Acheux; the main body travelled with the guns to the road between Bertrancourt and Beaussart.

Late in the evening we reached the position at Beaussart Railway Station, half-way between the village of that name and Bertrancourt. Here we took over from 59th Siege Battery, which was horse-drawn, meeting for the first time Mr. Grayson, who later became our Captain. Our guns were soon in action; in the café which we used as a C.P., the map was mounted and the arc drawn. We then carried on 59th Siege Battery's night task, and marked out an S.O.S. All that night it poured with rain, and everything was swamped. The roads and gun pits were flooded, and our clothes soaked through. We were lucky in finding huts with stoves in them near the guns. This good fortune, it is rumoured, was owing to our winning the toss for position with 195th Siege Battery!

The position was not a good one. We were on a crest hidden only by Colincamp's Ridge. Moreover, we were situated on a main road between two lines of railway. Such a position was delightful in times of "peace" for the R.O.D., who had erected numerous Nissen huts for their headquarters. There was an ample supply of water in the raised tanks, which had been used for supplying the engines. We used the before-mentioned Nissen huts at first, but these were not suitable as they afforded no protection from shrapnel or splinters, and were gradually removed by the R.E.'s. Some wooden shanties remained for our occupation, and we also used a large barn and three cellars for quarters. We found unoccupied a large and very strong surface dug-out which had been made in 1916, when the line ran as now on the Ancre, and soon after we arrived another of these fell vacant, and we took possession of it.

Our first business was to clean up our various quarters. Water from the surface well in the room behind the C.P. flowed over the floor and soaked down into the cellar below. Some drastic engineering reduced this discomfort, and some cleaning up made the C.P. habitable. Here and in other billets the stoves were kept burning brightly, and yielded a welcome warmth in the cold wet weather we were experiencing.

In our area the front line was as yet undetermined, but on 30th March New Zealand troops drove the Huns over the crest, capturing 3,000 yards of trench and taking 350 prisoners and some 110 machine guns. For a while we endured much heavy shelling, both H.E. and shrapnel landing in and around the position, without, however, doing any damage for the time being. We also were busy, and until counter-battery lists could be prepared by the Corps, strafed hostile lines of communication heavily. We were warned to expect an enemy push; indeed, the tenor of our instructions was defensive. The expected attack materialised on 5th April, a day on which the enemy deluged us with shrapnel. Three times he came over in mass formation, but failed to reach our trenches; on the third occasion he was met half-way by the New Zealand troops, who drove him back. This was the last Hun offensive on our front at Beaussart, but we were definitely advised of proposed advances for 13th April and 8th May. During the greater part of our stay in this position we were reckoning on a big German offensive, and it appears more than probable that the Hun was daily expecting us to attack. The offensives which we undertook were local, and designed to straighten the line at various points. The confidence of the New Zealanders in the success of projected raids was manifested in their operation orders, one of which commenced: " The New Zealanders will take the trench . . . ." Such confidence inspired confidence, and we entered into their plans with light hearts.

Our casualties during this period were not severe, yet we suffered more then than during the rest of our stay. On 5th April Gnr. T. Draper was wounded by shrapnel. The next day was our worst. A concentration of 4·2″ shells landed on the position, and one shell bursting close beside " C " gun, killed Gnr. E. P. Fryer outright. In him the battery lost a conscientious soldier and careful spotter. His body was buried in Beaussart Cemetery. The same day shells fell among the wooden huts behind the C.P., wounding B.S.M. G. W. Brassett and Gnr. J. G. Chisholme, the O.C.'s batman. Both were removed to hospital. On the 12th inst., Bmdr. B. Taylor was wounded in the hand by an anti-aircraft splinter, but resumed after being dressed and inoculated. Though we regretted these mischances of war, we congratulated ourselves that our casualties were so light.

In place of B.S.M. Brassett, Sergt. Turner was appointed Actg. B.S.M., and carried on for a month with conspicuous success until relieved by the posting of B.S.M. Harris to the battery. This worthy warrant officer showed a surprising activity in many directions; notably his method of checking the supply of Tubes on the guns evoked widespread admiration. One is led to believe—though an unlikely theory—that he suspected the " Number One" of "pinching" these as souvenirs.

On 6th April the battery lost Capt. Bennett, who was promoted to the command of 81st Siege Battery. In Capt. Bennett the battery had a most efficient and tireless officer; we missed his cheery and encouraging presence. To replace him Capt. Grayson joined us from 59th Siege Battery, and soon took his share of battery duties.

At this time, a scheme was devised and carried out to relieve the congestion at the position and secure the safety and comfort of the men. On 7th April arrangements were completed for billeting sections of the battery in a large house at Acheux. Here there was ample accommodation for the officers and men off duty. These billets were convenient in many ways. They were within easy reach of the position by either road or railway line, they were sufficiently roomy to allow of adequate sleeping space, they were compact, all the men being under one roof, and being in a small town where many troops were billeted, canteens were opened and frequent concerts were arranged in the Y.M.C.A. hut. Here, though we were within range of shells, and suffered from both H.E. and shrapnel, we were well content to remain, enjoying an occasional day in Doullens, reached by ration or other lorry, till the end of June, when the warm weather attracted us no less than the frequent shellings drove us to open-air billets on the road between Bus and Authie.

Soon there was a large number of heavy batteries of guns of all calibres in our vicinity. These shared with us the regular syn-chronised night-firng programmes devised to destroy hostile lines of communication, billet areas, dumps, etc. Airmen reported that this scheme was proving most effective. This is not to be wondered at, for the ammunition expenditure was enormous. We heard that the enemy had given up the use of roads for bringing up his supplies at night, so batteries were ordered to shell the tracks made by his carriers across the fields, which were clearly visible in the air photo-graphs. We know now that his supply of rations and material was greatly disorganised.

Soon the location of hostile batteries became sufficiently deter-mined for aeroplane shoots, and we did many destructive shoots with aeroplane observation, sometimes two in the day of 300 rounds each. Nor did we escape. Irregular concentrations burst over or around us without doing any real damage. On the night of 8th April a shell fell on the roof of our C.P., Gnr. Jackson, the machine gunner, having a narrow escape.

Our O.C. determined to secure a better position for the six guns, which were difficult to camouflage successfully in the open space they occupied. He selected a sunken road just behind the barn for the three guns of the Left Section, and found that the Right Section could be placed on the opposite side of the main road with a minimum of preparation and a maximum of safety from observing 'planes.

The sunken road chosen for the Left Section was too soft to move guns on, so out of our superabundance of railway sleepers, furnished by the old railhead platforms, we constructed a plank road some 50 yards long. The Left Section in this way had a platform along its whole length. There was also a double entrance dug-out built for this Section, made of sleepers throughout and giving about 20 feet of cover. The Right Section guns were sited amongst some old foundations on the other side of the road, and concealed most effectively by the broken nature of the ground, and camou-flaged to match their surroundings. A single entrance mined dug-out was made for the C.P. behind the Right Section, the mound being cleverly turfed by our gardening experts!

It contained a separate chamber for the telephone exchange, and beds for its occupants. It only lacked efficient ventilation. As soon as these necessary works were completed, our dug-out party began an addition to the officers' quarters. These already boasted a single chamber with one entrance, constructed in April by Bmdr. McLean and party, and to this was added another chamber at a lower level, with internal connecting staircase and a separate exit of 37 steps. The O.C.'s room at the lower level came last, and provided the acme of luxury! All this burrowing was rendered possible by our great store of sleepers, which also sufficed to provide the Brigade with 500.

Our dug-out squads varied, but amongst the many who did good work, the names of Cpl. Brown, Bmdrs. Evans, McLean, and

Nethercote, and Gnrs. Davies and Evans will be remembered, as well as those stalwart workers, Gnrs. Lee, O'Rourke, and Dan Sherman, the last-named showing renewed vigour when fortified by a second instalment of stew, or, failing that, a cup of " corfee!"

On 19th April, the Left Section was settled in the sunken road, the guns being registered the next day.

The Right Section moved on 3rd May after an aeroplane shoot carried out under conditions which involved a relay of men to transmit orders to the Left Section. The officer on duty had an afternoon's severe physical and vocal exercise as he shouted to the Right section or ran half-way to pass a correction to the Left. In the evening, the new C.P. was occupied, and we found it sufficiently roomy and very comfortable. It is probable that the amount of thorough work we expended on the new position saved us from a move to another part of the front.

We took part in several small attacks, all of which were successful. On 9th May the line of all guns was registered, officer and B.C.A. sitting in the open, above the dug-out, to enjoy the glorious sunshine. At this period the weather was magnificent, and the area so quiet that aeroplane shoots could be recorded on the famous mound under which the C.P. lay.

At this time permission was given to us to wear shorts, so long as we could do so without falling foul of the Ordnance. Many availed themselves of this privilege, though where the trousers thus mutilated came from need not be too closely enquired into. From the O.C. downward this fashion became the vogue, and whole detachments would turn out thus clad. The B.S.M. took to them as a duck takes to water, and proved his hardihood when the cold spells occurred, for he never would discard them, gaining for himself a nickname borrowed from a popular Army game!

Defensive preparations were still the keynote of our policy, and on 10th May the O.C. reconnoitred reserve positions to suit the selected reserve trench lines. We were also ordered to protect the battery with machine-gun emplacements and barbed wire defences in front. In fact, at this time barbed wire was the bane of our existence; not only must we wire to keep out the Hun, but the O.C. had wire laid to keep us off the grass, until the whole position was a perfect maze! We suspect that there was probably something in it, and it prevented tracks forming, but it certainly lengthened the journey to the cookhouse: at any rate "woe betide" anyone caught climbing over the wire!

On the 14th May the enemy strafed 12th Heavy Battery with 8″ shells, without inflicting either casualty or damage to guns. That battery was about 1,000 yards behind us, yet splinters and bases from the heavy shells fell over our position. On the day after, our No. 1 gun's camouflage took fire during a shoot, but after a few exciting moments was successfully extinguished by the prompt action of Sergt. Parnell and his detachment.

On the 17th there was a destructive shoot on our battery by 5·9 and 8″ artillery, but the enemy was 200 yards out in line. On 22nd May the O.C. granted permission to the men to be off duty one day in four, and the concession was very fully appreciated.

THE BATTERY POSITION AT BEAUSSART (Air Photograph).

The arrows point to the right and left "half battery" respectively, and indicate the "centre line."
The shell holes behind are those made by the eight-inch shoot on 12 Heavy Battery.

On the 24th Lieuts. Burroughs and Sunderland joined the battery. The former, who had been lecturing to officers at Lydd, suggested several improvements to expedite the working out of targets, and the B.C.A. staff prepared new books of tables, incorporating many of his ideas. Mr. Sunderland was an expert in camouflage, but could find no technical fault with the arrangements on that score, which, as aeroplane photographs show, hid the position and the guns almost perfectly. His sketching abilities utilised for O.P. panoramas and incidental happenings, have preserved many interesting pictures.

Three days later L/Bmdr. Robertson was wounded by a shrapnel bullet and removed to hospital.

Lieut. Green left us the day following (28th May), being transferred as Captain to 484th Siege Battery. Once again we lost a most efficient officer, whose knowledge and coolness were of distinct value to the battery.

Lieut.-Col. A. D. Murray left the Brigade about this time on his appointment to C.B.S.O., IX. Corps. All greatly regretted his departure. He was succeeded by Lieut.-Col. A. C. Wilkinson, C.M.G., D.S.O., who retained command of the Brigade until the end of this history.

The week during which the changes of the preceding paragraphs were taking place was prolific of renewed rumours of a great Hun offensive. These rumours were sedulously fostered by the home Press, and increased hostile artillery activity, marked for us by the shelling of our billets at Acheux (26th May), and of Doullens Railway Station, seemed to lend probability to them. Whatever this renewed activity portended, it was not followed by any forward infantry move on our front.

With June came multiple aeroplane shoots, when, according to official reports, we destroyed one hostile battery position after another. In this month also the Balloon Section observed shoots for us. One evening, as we were carrying on a shoot under balloon observation, a 'plane called us up, and we had the almost unique experience of carrying through two shoots at one time. Had it not been for a line to the Left Section, recently laid, over which we could transmit orders by telephone, such a performance would have been almost impossible. As it was, both shoots passed off successfully. During such shoots hostile artillery frequently opened neutralising fire on our area, though usually to our right flank; but by the simple subterfuge of ceasing fire while it continued, we secured ourselves from too unwelcome attentions and interruptions. 'Planes called us up frequently in the evening. On 6th June, we began a 300-round shoot at 5 p.m.; on the 26th we commenced another of the same at 7.15 p.m. On these occasions the 'plane ranged the guns, and left the fire for effect to our own judgment. Another change in the battery personnel occurred on the 24th, when Lieut. G. A. Smith left us to take up duty as Orderly Officer at Brigade H.Q. For the time being Mr. Smith remained on the strength of the battery, and we were pleased to think that an authority on sport of all sorts, who was so popular an officer, was not entirely lost to us.

Towards the end of the month "flu" became rampant among the Signallers, who had made themselves at home in the old C.P. and Station House. Within three days fourteen of them were removed to hospital, but most of them rejoined later. Of those who were posted from the Base to other batteries, Signaller J. Buchan, who had long been the liveliest and most energetic of a busy bunch, was killed about a month before the Armistice brought an end to hostilities. The gun detachments suffered less severely, though several men were removed to hospital. The officers, among whom Padre Newell had taken up his quarters, had a bad time, too, for five of them, including the Padre, were laid up on the same day (3rd July).

The billets at Bus were now completed. Each sub-section had built its own shelter, digging a pit from which the loose material was banked up to form a protection against splinters. A super-structure of wood and corrugated iron shielded the occupants from the weather. Further protection and camouflage were secured by building these wooden cabins close into a wooded bank, which hid also the officers' mess and sleeping tents. Altogether the billets were admirably placed, and our days in the open there were most enjoyable. A lorry carried the men to and from the position, though many preferred to walk. At billets, the battery canteen worked at high pressure. We were very close to the Balloon Section in the wood alongside, and our most exciting time was when the balloon was brought down by shrapnel on the evening of 9th July, for the showers of bullets fell over us!

Under the more settled warfare of this period, extra leaves were granted to the battery for officers and men who were war-weary, or were not due for Blighty leave for a long time. By the two schemes, some officers and n.c.o.'s had a good rest at St. Valerie, and one n.c.o. and gunner were lucky enough to get "French" leave, during which the former had a golden week in Paris and the latter a glorious time around Le Havre. It was unfortunate that large numbers could not benefit under these excellent schemes, but perhaps the war conditions or the position on our immediate front did not admit of larger allotments of these invigorating breaks from the nervous strain of action.

On the evening of 17th July there was a trench raid, and the wonderful lights with which the enemy filled the sky were never seen to better advantage. During the months of June and July we had many gas alarms, and were ordered to wear our respirators for practice for an hour on several successive evenings. This prompt action kept us on the alert, and no cases of gassing were reported in the battery. In June also the O.C. had a field day with the men off duty. They practised skirmishing in open order against an imaginary enemy, who fortunately remained intangible.

We had a visit from six officers of 299th Siege Battery on 23rd July. They said they were taking over our position—our first warning that we were likely to pull out. They were both astonished and pleased with the arrangements we had made, and delighted to know we had escaped observation by hostile 'planes. When the time arrived a week later for our departure, we left Beaussart with keen regret. We had done much good work, but for the most part it had been performed under conditions which in many respects were ideal.

No chapter on our stay at Beaussart would be complete without mention of the part played by the signallers. Once the lines had been laid to Brigade, sister batteries, and O.P.'s, their work at the position was practically over. It was at the O.P. that their hardest days were spent. Constant shelling of the roads made the journeys exciting, as constant breaking of the lines made the life of the linesmen strenuous and their labours unending. Then there were lines to be laid out to, and reeled in from, the forward O.P.'s in the trenches, where the telephonists picked up news of all sorts from the infantry. We must mention, too, the famous half-way house on the far side of Mailly Maillet, where they were frequently held up for a time by barrage fire before proceeding to Auchonvillers. Strange to say we discovered and used the system of buried lines that had been laid for the 1916 offensive, and in turn our signallers and gunners buried a line to the O.P. known as Apple Trees. At this pill-box O.P. the telephonists at first occupied a corrugated iron shed, close to which a 5·9 dud buried itself one day. They discovered at this place the 1916 dug-out, but shortly afterwards a 4·2″ shell, bursting near where the 5·9 dud had fallen, blew up the entrance. Of the lighter side of their life we can tell only of the fine time some of them had with "scrounged" vin blanc at Mailly Maillet, hint at the fine suppers they prepared, chiefly from potatoes, and call to memory Buchan's cow tethered outside the cellar and regularly milked by the lanky Scotsman in the mornings, till it was stolen in turn by the New Zealanders, who removed it from our vicinity for their own benefit.

DEPARTURE FROM BEAUSSART.

Our departure from Beaussart was very hurried. On the 30th July, at about mid-day, we got orders to prepare to move that night to an unknown destination, but that our first halt was to be at Vauchelles, where billets were to be arranged by an advance party. Stores were accordingly packed, and all preparations made for departure, which entailed the abandonment of numerous useful articles we had collected during our four months in that position.

On several evenings previous to our pulling out, gas concentrations had been fired on and around our positions, but though the column was forced to remain for an hour in the Beaussart-Bertrancourt Road, no hostile activity interfered with the operations.

The battery moved out at dusk, and on arrival at Vauchelles, billetted in a barn and several houses at the cross roads.

The next day was treated as something of a holiday, and many took advantage of the near neighbourhood of cafés and estaminets, some, we fear, supping, perhaps not unwisely, but at any rate a little too well.

On the morning of the 1st August there was a lecture by the O.C., which all ranks had to attend, on "Camouflage and Concealment of Battery Positions"—these things will happen! That day

4.

also we took a whole lorry load of superfluous stores and left them in charge of the Ordnance.

Having received our orders, we left Vauchelles at 9.15 in the evening and, travelling through Marieux, Puichvillers, and Renevillers, reached Longpré, on the outskirts of Amiens, at 1.30 a.m. on the 2nd August. The billetting party had met with no success, and the only shelter from the rain was a "Dutch" barn with open sides. That night, for the first time, we heard the crash in Amiens of the great 11″ shells with which the Hun was bombarding the city. Heavy rain fell all day on the 2nd, but we were able to get billets for that night and slept well.

On the evening of 3rd August we were again on the move, and had the interesting experience of travelling the deserted streets of Amiens, until so recently the centre of attraction and the Mecca of every man on the Western Front.

CHAPTER X.
THE BATTLE OF AMIÈNS.

Marshall Foch's blows against the enemy were to develop rapidly all along the line. To relieve the tension following the already-expended threat against Amiens, and as the first move in the British offensive, an attack in which French, Canadian, and Australian troops were to participate was carefully prepared on the Villers Bretonneux front. To our Brigade fell the part of supporting the Canadian Corps.

Reconnaisance for a position at Gentelles, to the south-east of Villers Bretonneux, was ordered by Brigade and carried out. Over 1,500 rounds of ammunition had been taken there over bad roads—so bad, indeed, that four separate parties were organised in the battery to travel by different routes to the new position.

It was a very dark night, and the complicated arrangements, no less than the next-to-impossible roads, made the movement difficult. The O.C. called at Brigade, where he heard that the Gentelles position was cancelled, and was ordered to retrieve his parties, turn round, and draw in at some convenient place on the Amiens-Villers-Bretonneux Road, and await further instructions. This change of plan had to be undertaken while the converging parties were still "en route"; the guns must be turned on narrow roads; the new resting place must be chosen in a darkness that could almost be felt.

In such circumstances we were fortunate in finding a short but very suitable loop-road beside an R.E. dump, about a mile from Villers Bretonneux. The weather was fine, and ignoring the dampness of the ground, we found our kits and slept in the open until awakened in the early morning by the firing of a 6″ Mark XIX. gun at our very ears. We discovered our exact position on the map—reference over the dump (N29d24)—and here we remained till 6th August, more or less happy despite the broken weather, in discovered dug-outs or temporary shelters under gun sheets. Hours were spent by some of us in endless but futile discussion and speculation suggested by the constant stream of traffic and transport along the road as to our next movement. But we were not long left in doubt.

Our Brigade was ordered to select positions in the Bois l'Abbaie. The four O.C.'s found that almost all possible positions in the wood were already occupied, and though our sister battery (195) and the two heavy batteries found positions there, our battery was forced beyond it. Hence we were the foremost heavy battery—a place of honour we held throughout the battle, adding pride of time to that of place by being the first to move up when moving became feasible, and the earliest to open fire.

On the night of 6th August the guns were moved forward to Villers Bretonneux, where we occupied the selected position in a field of corn behind the village, the guns being camouflaged as corn stacks until the time to open fire arrived. On this and the preceding evening the enemy shelled very heavily in our area, and we were most fortunate in escaping casualties. Next day telephonic communication was established with Brigade and O.P. (on the railway bridge), and in the evening the infantry moved up to their assembly positions. Our position was rather forcibly brought home to two of the officers who, while making a little motor tour forward, were warned to keep their heads down! By dusk, ammunition for the bombardment was in readiness at the guns, while in the commodious cellar of a house which we nick-named "Bairnsfather Villa," the several targets were worked out, and the officer on duty wrote out instructions for each No. 1.

Our targets exhibited a novel phase of counter-battery work. Until then it had been usual to put one or more batteries against a known hostile battery; on this occasion our five guns were laid on five different hostile batteries, and other British and Colonial batteries being similarly disposed, an effective cross-fire was secured on the one hand, while on the other errors in laying out the line of the guns were less likely to render any enemy position immune from our fire. The line of ours and all the other batteries was laid out on the new Field Survey picket system, which had recently come into vogue with such excellent results.

During the night the Germans shelled the village and surrounding areas, as usual, a concentration of pip-squeaks falling around us; but though unfortunately they played havoc in a Tank park, we had little reason to suspect they had the faintest anticipation of the surprise we had prepared for them, or that it would be necessary for us to "open on counter preparation lines." At the same time our speculations on these points added to the excitement of the occasion. From time to time this nervous excitement became intense. There was little sleep for anybody, and most of us lay in the open.

Close upon Zero hour (4.20 a.m.) the O.C., with one or two officers, was on the position. Watch in hand, he held the attention of all. There was a tense silence, in which we heard the Nos. 1 of surrounding batteries reporting in turn as our O.C. counted off the seconds remaining. When these had slipped by, the order "Fire," coinciding with that on neighbouring batteries, relieved the tension. It was not yet dawn.

A terrific salvo, from what seemed like thousands of guns, announced the opening of the offensive, and to us at least the surprise to the enemy troops seemed perfect. From 4.20 to 9.20 o'clock on the morning of the glorious 8th August, we continued to drive a constant flight of shells on hostile battery positions in terms of an operation order that worked to the second for the greater part of the time. Reports from our F.O.O. were extremely favourable, and our only casualty occurred early in the bombardment, when a premature on an 18-pounder gun near by wounded Gnr. Greaves in the face. The German reply to our fire was feeble to the vanishing point. Shells fell on and near the bridge which carries the main road over the railway track, but it was impossible in such a din to hear the flight or even the crash of hostile shells; only by seeing the bursts and answering the dozen N.F. calls sent by airmen could one know that our fire was being returned. Captured guns told their own story; many were loaded but had not been fired; their positions were destroyed.

We had had little to smoke throughout the night, and less to eat. For once in a way Army biscuits were at a premium. Breakfast came as a most pleasant break. Meanwhile the rapidity of the German retreat permitted the dispatch of our advanced section, a position for which had been reconnoitred at 7.30 a.m. by the O.C. The gunners who accompanied him had much to tell on their return. About 9 o'clock " E " and " F " guns went forward to the point selected south-west of Marcelcave, then moved further to Cayeux, whence the section was ordered back to another position north-east of Marcelcave. No firing occurred in any of these positions, and the pre-arranged system of ground strips, by which the airmen would know the calibre and number of guns and number of rounds of ammunition at their disposal, proved abortive, for the section was not called up. Owing to this failure, no less than to the uncertainty of the line in such a fast-moving battle, the forward section had not fired before the remainder of the guns came up in the evening.

While the forward section moved off, the remaining guns fired on targets selected by the O.C., the progress of the battle having made the normal programme impossible of completion. When " cease fire " was ordered at 9.20 a.m., those remaining behind rested for the most part by the main road, along which large parties of prisoners and small quantities of material of war were being brought back. By 5 o'clock the F.W.D.'s were loaded, and all set off in good spirits to join the forward party, " A " gun, which had been at Workshops, now being brought up to complete our strength.

Travelling along the shell-holed roads through the war-destroyed and German-rifled villages of Warfusee, Abancourt and Marcelcave (where we first came into touch with the forward party) to that of Wiencourt, where the battery was re-united, we took up position and got into action on the west of the village. Next day we fired towards noon on the still-retreating enemy, who was, however, still shelling our vicinity. In the afternoon we moved forward to Guillaucourt. The guns were pulled in along a bank near the railway, but though we got smartly into action, no firing took place. Some of the men hunting soldier-wise for souvenirs found a German incoming mail, which was, however, more useful to the Intelligence Department of the Army than to the finders.

It was here that we saw one of our own observation balloons brought down in flames by the machine-gun fire of a British S.E. 5 machine, carrying British identification marks. The observers made a safe descent by means of their parachutes, but the balloon was destroyed. The incident was immediately reported to Brigade, but we never discovered whether the aeroplane, which was accompanied by two others of similar make and markings, was thought to have been piloted by a German, or whether some of our own 'planes mistook the balloon for an enemy, owing to its advanced position in the confusion of moving warfare.

In the evening tents were erected for C.P. and Wireless, but the familiar sounds of German 'planes overhead, accompanied by the no less familiar noise of bursting bombs, made the early night uncomfortable. Orders to stand by at midnight introduced in the darkness an element of confusion, dispelled shortly afterwards by a countermanding order that breakfast would be served at 3.30 a.m. After a short period of repose stores were loaded with praiseworthy rapidity and, considering the veto on lights, absence of confusion, and the whole cavalcade was "en route " by daybreak. Early morning found us on the road to Caix (on this stretch the circumventing of a derelict Tank astride the road was successfully carried out). Through this village we pushed to Rosieres, with the debris of a recent hard struggle on all sides.

At this village, which had fallen the previous evening (9th August) our guns were drawn in near the cemetery to the north of the village. We got into action by 8 a.m., and opened fire in support of a further advance by the Canadians, the only heavy battery to take part. We took pride in this achievement, and felt fully repaid for the exertions of the previous days.

The Germans had left behind large stores, and many valuable instruments, maps, papers, and letters fell into our hands. Indiscriminate souvenir-hunting, accompanied by wanton destruction, led to the loss of valuable material, and finally a guard was mounted over the stores. Still more necessary was the guard over the drink discovered by the troops. At the same time the exploration of a Germany canteen added artificial honey (Kunsthonig) and barley sugar to a monotonous dietary, and the discovery of cases of German blacking was evidenced by occasional pairs of brightly polished boots.

During the first part of our stay at Rosieres, we fired frequently, and a nightly harassing fire was maintained on the enemy's lines of communication, etc. The Germans were making a stand on their 1916 line, from which, however, we dislodged them later. Meanwhile the early appearance of a Canadian Y.M.C.A. relieved our discomforting shortage of cigarettes by a free issue of two per man, while it allowed those who were fortunate enough to have a few francs left to purchase a few luxuries, such as chocolate and biscuits.

A more advanced position was selected near Meharicourt, but although ammunition was dumped for future use, this position was never occupied. A guard was mounted over the dump, and found the dug-out near by more than useful in the frequent shelling to which the area was subjected. On one occasion the sheltering guard missed one of its members, who was discovered busy in the branches of an apple tree, where some fruit had escaped the notice or attention of previous sentries!

On 15th August we became a silent battery and, with the exception of a few rounds at extreme range for purposes of registration, observed by the O.C. from the excellent vantage point in the church tower, when some French officers watched our bursts and admired the accuracy of our fire, and a few harassing rounds from " E " gun in the afternoon on which we pulled out, life at Rosieres was fairly easy and comparatively unexciting.

During this rest period we were ordered to form a complete battery of German 8″ (20 c.m.) and 5·9″ (15 c.m.) Howitzers and guns. Examination of the scattered pieces showed that the 8″ Howitzers had been stripped of all moveable parts, and that not one could be fired. We secured one 5·9″ gun and four 5·9″ Howitzers, transported them by caterpillars to a position near Meharicourt, and got them into action. A detachment was detailed to go and fire them, and the line was laid by means of our own dial sights. We were able to observe from the position both air and ground bursts. The detachment found the Howitzers easy to handle, but their short range was a matter of comment for some days, while the range of the gun—about 20,000 metres—was a change after our own comparatively short-range Howitzers.

Hostile aircraft were very active during these days at Rosières, and we watched several air fights. One, in which we watched a British aeroplane, evidently piloted by a crack performer, bring down two Huns within three minutes; and another, a mighty battle in which over fifty 'planes were engaged, and in which two falling Hun machines disgorged their pilots hanging from toy-like parachutes.

Hostile shellings were short and came at irregular intervals, gas shells keeping us on the alert at night. Our only casualty befell us on 18th August, when Gnr. Giddings, one of the original members of the battery, was unfortunately wounded in the leg by a splinter whilst acting as spotter. Nor were the night prowling raiding 'planes more successful, though inadvertency in firing the guns while these bombers were overhead brought some half-dozen bombs in unpleasant proximity to the position. Most of the men made themselves comfortable in houses with cellars or in shallow dug-outs and, benefitting by most propitious weather conditions, all took the opportunity of cleaning up for the next move.

On 27th August the French took over on our front. As they marched along the roads in the moonlight keeping cautiously among the shadows to escape the notice of the hostile airmen, they presented a picturesque appearance to the few onlookers. Their entry was the prelude to our exit, and the excellent news from other parts of the front produced a most cheerful spirit among us all. We anticipated our transference to the front on which the relieved Canadians were now installed. For us the Battle of Amiens was over: we regarded it as an excellent piece of staff work; we were proud of our share in an irresistible push; everything augured well for our next blow against the Hun.

Tangible recognition of the excellence of our work throughout the battle was forthcoming later. For his valuable services to the battery as liason officer with the infantry, Lieut. Johnson was awarded the Military Cross—a decoration which unfortunately he was destined never to wear. Well deserved Military Medals were conferred on Sergt. Turner, Sergt. Parnell, and Sergt. Nicholls.

CHAPTER XI.

BATTLE OF ARRAS.

I.—THE QUEANT DROCOURT SWITCH.

We pulled out from Rosières on the evening of 27th August, and retraced our way to Wiencourt, where the destroyed houses, around the defiled church with its desecrated vaults, became our billets. The next day was wet, and several of the men found a fine sleeping place in the huge cellars of a large house. On the following day we again set off in our lorries still further over known roads through Villers Bretonneux to Cagny, where we found good billets in the village, which, though it was partly evacuated by its inhabitants, bore few traces of war. A canteen added to our comfort, and we renewed our stocks of canteen goods. Many enjoyed bathing in the river; games of cricket and football were played.

Rumours as to our destination were rife and, following a story that we had missed being sent to Italy by the spin of a coin, Russia was suggested and found some supporters! Doubts and fears were set at rest when, after 5.30 a.m. breakfast on 31st August, we paraded at 9 to move off to Arras. The guns with their detachments, the stores with the cooks and the officers entrained at Longueau about 9 p.m., the men being accommodated in the regulation horse boxes, which, except for a small part in the centre, were inches deep in manure, that had to be removed. A small party travelled by road in the lorries. In the early morning the two parties were within hail of one another at Frevent, and the battery was reunited at St. Catherines to the north of Arras in the early afternoon.

Here billets had been arranged for us, but orders coming in, we set off almost immediately. We passed through the battered city of Arras, about twelve months having elapsed since our guns and lorries had previously travelled through. Few civilians were in the city, but it was now a centre of military activity.

After the first few days of the Battle of Amiens, the Canadian Corps had been withdrawn and sent to another part of the front. What that front was we did not then know, but we were soon to find that we were rejoining that famous Corps for one of those great pushes with which Marshall Foch was defeating the Hun. We believe we are right in saying that the success of the Canadian Corps in these repeated pushes was due not only to the excellent fighting qualities which they possessed, but also to the fact that they were able to keep their divisions at full strength, in spite of the heavy casualties they suffered, from the large reserve of reinforcements which lay at their disposal.

During our journey towards the Arras front, heavy fighting had been taking place. Bullecourt and the Wotan Switch Line had already fallen, and further advances were in preparation. It was evident from the great quantities of war material with which Arras was packed, that we were in for another big battle. We soon found that there were many batteries in the line, and the arrival of our Brigade further reinforced them. Our next halt was at Agny, where we parked the column of guns and lorries facing our probable line of advance. Here we found what shelter we could in tents, and the old abandoned shelters of a line of disused trenches.

We learned that evening that a great attack was planned for the morrow, no less than the crossing of the Queant-Drocourt Switch, a formidable obstacle and the last stronghold of the Hindenburg system of trenches.

Next morning breakfast was served between 3.30 and 4 a.m. We stood by until about 11 o'clock, watching in the early hours the flashes of the opening bombardment, in which we had not been required to take part. Receiving orders to advance, the whole Brigade moved forward, and soon we reached the battle ground over which prisoners and wounded were already passing back.

The O.C. had orders to select a position in the open valley beyond Eterpigny. He had set off with Major Wilson, of 195th Siege Battery, in the battery car, but found the village suffering under annihilating shell fire. Through this they dashed, meeting difficulties in the form of fallen trees and many dead bodies. After several unsuccessful attempts to discover the road to the selected area, they found a narrow, deeply-sunken, but sheltered road, where the car could be left near a lorry that had found cover there. From this point the two O.C.'s pushed forward on foot into the valley until they met a major of the Machine Gun Corps, who, in answer to their startling statement that they were selecting positions for heavy artillery, told them that an infantry struggle for the valley was in progress, and that the machine-guns were not there yet. Heavy artillery was, therefore, out of the question. Just then a hostile artillery strafe broke out, and the O.C.'s returned to the sunken road, where they found the car driver ruefully examining a puncture in the front, and a four-foot iron wiring corkscrew in the back tyre. Shell fire of uncanny accuracy and persistence opened on the sunken road, and under this repairs had to be carried out. The lorry men of the sheltering F.S.C. lorry had lost their officer, and were waiting dejectedly in a hole for his return. The sunken road was barricaded with German ammunition boxes, and there was nothing for it but to return through Eterpigny, where the shelling resembled a cloud burst. Through this inferno they came unscathed, taking corners on two wheels. An alternative position behind Eterpigny was found to be hopeless, so they came back to provisional Brigade H.Q., where they found the Colonel at a very "unhealthy" spot on the Arras-Cambrai road just beyond Vis-en-Artois. They received orders to return along the road towards Arras, meet the advancing Brigade, and tell all the batteries to turn round and get off the road without interfering with the two continuous streams of traffic. This was a peculiarly difficult operation, because about three miles of the main road, on which the guns were, passed through a shelled area, with no level ground on to which the batteries could be drawn to await a possible forward move. The root of the trouble was that our advance had not been so rapid as the Staff had hoped.

We had pushed forward to the Arras-Cambrai road, where the order to move back was given. On the return journey a stray shell bursting near by killed two men and wounded Lieuts. Archer and Bloye, the former being removed to hospital, the latter, after inoculation, resuming with the battery. While we were awaiting further orders, biscuits and bully were issued at 6 p.m.—our first meal since 4 a.m.

"E" and "F" guns were ordered forward to occupy a position alongside a balloon section in a hollow on the roadside where they were to stand by for S.O.S., the remaining four guns returned to Agny, where we had spent the preceding night. By morning the attack had developed sufficiently for our guns to proceed, and a position for "A" and "B" guns, which had come up, was selected along the Arras-Cambrai road, beyond the ruins of Haucourt. "E" and "F" guns were drawn in alongside "A" and "B" in the course of the day.

Our new position, from which we fired at once, suffered in the hostile road strafing, and only the securing of a strong sap under the road saved the battery from casualties. During the night several bombs fell so close as to seem on top of us, and transport and horses were not so fortunate as we, packed though we were, like sardines along the sap and on the steps leading to both exits. Few of us will ever forget that night. Three of the signallers passed the night in a small elephant-iron shelter about 100 yards from the road, and declare that except for a little wakefulness, when the aforementioned bombs were dropped, and when horse transport passed over their shelter, missing the entrance by a few inches only, they passed a fairly comfortable night!

It was for his promptitude, coolness, and resource in extinguishing some Hun small arm ammunition that had been set on fire by hostile shells, and was very close to our ammunition, that Cpl. J. Brown received the Military Medal.

The next morning (4th September), "E" and "F" guns were moved forward to the cross roads at Villers-les-Cagnicourt (known to the battery for several weeks as "Hell-fire Corner"), taking up position and getting into action in a field just west of the Saudemont road.

While the O.C. was at H.Q. news came through that enemy traffic was congesting the Douai-Cambrai road and the railway junction at Aubencheul. He heard orders given to the 60-pounders to disperse the traffic. No 6″ Howitzers were sufficiently far advanced to reach these inviting targets. So, anxious on one hand to engage the traffic and on the other to remove his men from the heavily strafed line of communication of the Arras-Cambrai road, he asked for permission to go forward for the express purpose of shooting at the railway junction. This was granted, and in the afternoon "A" and "B" guns had a rapid journey (owing to hostile road shelling) by Hell-Fire Corner along the road to Recourt, turning off on a dry weather track which let us pass to the south of Saudemont and strike the road to Rumaucourt, near the village. Our position was most picturesque, the guns being well camouflaged in a small orchard on the west of the village, while German ammunition shelters well built and stoutly floored made excellent quarters for us all.

We knew we were still in front of the Field Artillery, but were much surprised to learn from some infantrymen that between us and the enemy were only a few outposts!

Our advance was being held up at the Canal du Nord and Canal de la Sensee, and we were waiting for a new push. Meanwhile we harassed roads, and under aeroplane observation, harassed batteries. Nor did we escape, for both sections were subjected to shelling at odd intervals, fortunately with no serious results as yet. "E" and "F" guns were moved up to Saudemont, and had a hotter time there than the forward section experienced at Rumaucourt.

Meanwhile, the remaining guns and the Q.M.S. stores had come forward to the old position on the Arras-Cambrai road, where, however, hostile shelling made life more exciting than restful. The concentration of guns, stores, personnel, etc., along the Arras-Cambrai road resembled a peace-time manœuvre ground. Doubtless this was smartly spotted by enemy 'planes, and it was from the consequent area shoots that we suffered. The balloon section, which had moved forward alongside us, was treated very severely, losing many balloons and suffering heavy casualties in personnel. Additional weakness lay in the nearness of the Arras-Cambrai road to our left flank, on which we were acting on the defensive, sufficiently protected by the Sensee River and swamps. Our later billets were more satisfactory, because they were further to our right. In the dark night of 4-5th September it was considered advisable to move from that unhealthy spot, and new billets were stumbled on in a line of trenches running off the Hendecourt Road.

Even these billets did not escape from enemy shell fire; shells that were evidently intended for the road flung splinters over the billet area, but for some time one heard only of hairbreadth escapes. The journey by lorry to and from the positions was always exciting for the gun reliefs. The Germans strafed the road heavily, and we had the idea that the songs sung "en route" were not altogether the outflow of joyful hearts. At the same time the rapid travelling over rough roads made the journey uncomfortable in the extreme, and many old bones found the jolting trying and tiring.

Of the incidents at these Hendecourt billets we have space for only two. One day the road subsided near the cookhouse, resulting in an underlying dug-out being demolished, fortunately without any dire consequences. The vicinity of the billet area was covered with low bilberry bushes which were rich in fruit. It occurred to us one day to gather a large quantity of the berries, and the cooks prepared and served bilberry pie, a most welcome variation to the usual rice or oatmeal preparation that has become so inseparable from the Army dinner.

Our good fortune in escaping unscathed from hostile shells at these three positions continued unbroken, till towards the end of our occupation. "C" and "D" guns had been brought up to Rumaucourt from billets and put in position alongside "A" and "B." It seemed certain that a further advance had been planned. Meanwhile several aeroplane shoots had been carried through, both at Saudemont and, following the transference of the wireless apparatus and staff to the East Section on 23rd September, at Rumaucourt. These shoots took place under trying conditions—enemy 'planes were troublesome, and intermittent hostile shelling, followed frequently by gas shelling or bombing at night, kept us all on the " qui vive."

During this interesting period of more settled warfare the battery suffered casualties in each of the three positions. We lost several good friends, though fortunately most of them will be able to resume their civil employment.

Mr. Bloye was hit by a splinter whilst on O.P. duty (the second time in a fortnight) though not so severely as to prevent him taxing Bmdr. Taffs' pedestrian powers to the utmost on the way to the dressing station. He recovered to return to the battery at a later date, not included in the scope of this history.

Even at billets, as we have noted, shell splinters whizzed uncomfortably close. On 10th September, as we were digging holes in which to sink the tents, we had to shelter in the trench for a few minutes, and bombs were dropped in the vicinity that night. On 12th September, Gnr. T. H. Wilson, who had just returned from leave, was wounded in the legs by splinters as he lay in his bivouac. Following this untoward incident, and taking advantage of the evacuation of some good dug-outs by their occupants, tents were dispensed with, and we secured safer cover underground or in more substantially built shelters till we in turn moved our billets forward.

Saudemont was the hottest position throughout our stay in that area. The village suffered severely both by day and night, and it was necessary to drive the ration lorry carefully over its shell-hole-pitted streets, on which house walls were occasionally blown by shell fire, and dead horses proved awkward obstacles. Altogether our life here was unenviable. Shelling was a daily occurrence, because the Germans used the village church as a convenient registration point for their guns, and in addition fired regular concentrations on the village and its approaches. During one of these concentrations, on 25th September, several 5·9 shells (H.E. and gas) fell close to the C.P. and Wireless Cellars, one bursting on the roof above the latter and wounding Whlr.-Sergt. T. B. Stringer, Staff-Sergt. J. Cunningham and Gnr. J. Pole. Staff-Sergt. Cunningham, after having his wound dressed, rejoined the section, though he limped badly for several days; the others went to hospital. On the night of 16th September a hostile bombing raid added to our list of casualties in a strange manner. A bomb fell outside the Signallers' cellar, and a splinter entering the front door and flying down the cellar steps ricochetted from wall to wall before striking Signaller P. H. Brown in the face as he lay on the floor of the cellar.

At Rumaucourt, too, we were shelled and bombed irregularly, and experienced several short but sharp gas concentrations. From this position we used to watch the shells bursting on Saudemont, and compare out lot with that of our comrades there. Here, also, the section had been doing good work. During a part of the time we were supposed to answer only ANF calls, but night-firing targets and aeroplane shoots still came in regularly. We had no more than commenced a destructive shoot on 24th September, after a few datuming rounds, than neutralising fire was opened on the battery position. However, we completed ranging, and when, after we had fired some of our rounds for effect, the 'plane gave CI, we broke off for dinner, but just as Lieut. Johnson joined the men to examine the guns after the shelling to which they had been subjected, a shell burst on the position killing him outright and wounding Ftr.-S.S. J. J. Gorst, Sergt. W. Turner, and Gnr. W. White. Gnr. White died at the dressing station in the early evening. Mr. Johnson and he lie side by side in a little roadside cemetery near Haucourt, on the Arras-Cambrai road.

In Mr. Johnson the battery lost one of its best officers. His interest in the men gained him the respect of all ranks, and we keenly felt his death. He had been through the mill with us since the dark Ribecourt days, and had done his best for the efficiency of the battery.

The next morning a shell fell right under the muzzle of "A" gun, but most fortunately for all concerned it proved a "dud."

The Battle of Arras was now passing into the great offensive all along the line. The Germans had made a stiff resistance along the canals, but signs were not wanting that our advance was shortly to be resumed. We felt that with the return of the O.C. from leave (26th September) we could face the trials and problems of this great forward sweep with our customary confidence and cheerfulness.

On the same date Lieut. Mockridge was added to the strength of the battery.

CHAPTER XII.

THE BATTLE OF ARRAS.

II.—THE CANALS.

The Canal du Nord was the next obstacle to overcome. It was too strongly held to permit of a frontal attack, and the offensive had to be developed from a flank. A weak spot near Moeuvres—famous in the annals of this war—was chosen for the initial attack.

By midnight, 26-27th September, we had received our allotted targets for this new effort, and at 5.20 a.m. on the morning of the 27th our guns opened out in company with vast numbers of others which had been brought up. The whole area within range beyond the Canal was systematically and thoroughly prepared for the infantry attack.

The distinguishing feature of this battle was that it was a swing round from right to left, the principal crossing of the Canal being on the extreme right of the front attacked. Once the crossing was safely effected, it was expected that the defences of the Canal thus "turned" would be rolled up with comparative ease. This actually happened, one division being detailed for this clearing up duty, while others which had crossed from Moeuvres deployed on to an ever-widening arc.

Our battery positions were at about the centre of the arc described, and it follows that the distance to the barrage line did not greatly increase. We were thus able to follow the progress of the operations by noticing the position of the smoke from the barrage. The time table was strictly maintained.

At 11 a.m. the Colonel, accompanied by the O.C. and Capt. Le Lievre, of the 12th Heavy Battery, proceeded on a reconnaissance of possible battery positions to the bridge at Marquion, where the Arras -Cambrai road crosses the Canal. It was here that a part of that division detailed for the clearing up of the Canal was to cross. They found this not yet accomplished. Marquion was still full of machine-guns, which commanded the crossing and prevented the R.E.'s from beginning the work of throwing a temporary bridge across. Under shell and machine-gun fire, pontoons were being brought up and much other material—duckboards on cork floats, brushwood for crossing the swamps, etc. The infantry who were to cross were waiting their opportunity, taking cover where they could in ditches and behind trees, while their advance parties of snipers, machine-gunners, and temporary bridge experts were pushing on through the swamps which lie about the edges of the Canal. They were shortly afterwards successful, assisted by the advancing infantry sweeping up from Moeuvres.

Many exciting incidents in this day's struggle were witnessed from our observation posts, which commanded a view of a great part of the battle area. As illustrating the rapid progress of our advance, one series may be mentioned in which the battle passed from advanced skirmishers to artillery in twelve minutes. Scene: a field with a wood in front and a road leading to a village behind—German riflemen in pits in a field—a sudden charge of fifty British infantry—some of the Huns bolt while others make a fight for it—hand-to-hand fighting all over the field—some running, some wounded, some killed, the remainder made prisoners. Next a steady stream of our infantry across the field and up the road to the village in hot pursuit. These have hardly disappeared and the prisoners been marched away before a battery is unlimbering in the field, and within twelve minutes of our first contact with the enemy is in action and firing.

The Canal du Nord was cleared, and the villages on the other side one by one fell into our hands, the last to fall being Oisy-le-Verger, which, when the barrage reached it, looked on its hill like a volcano in eruption. By 6 o'clock in the evening we had fired thirteen hundred rounds from our two positions, and had escaped without casualty. The enemy reply had not been considerable so far as we were concerned beyond some rather brisk shelling on Saudemont in the opening hours of the attack.

The series of battles which began at Arras and resulted in the fall of Cambrai left a long left flank exposed. This left flank became longer with each advance of the line towards Cambrai. It was a flank of great natural strength, being formed by marshes of the Sensee River—in places nearly a mile wide—but it had to be defended and troops provided for the purpose. The tactics of this defended left flank were obviously sound, as by driving in a long protected wedge towards Cambrai we eventually compelled the Huns to clear out of the pocket left by our advance. In spite of its tactical soundness, the shape of this front put everyone to vast inconvenience, for our main line of communication, the Arras-Cambrai road, was, along most of its length, within range of the German heavy artillery on the left.

After the Battle of the Canal du Nord, which was entirely successful and took our infantry into the outskirts of Cambrai, we remained to guard this left flank and to neutralise by our fire the German batteries covering it. Shortly after this, the 22nd Corps, who had taken the chief part in the Battle of the Canal du Nord, were relieved by the Canadians, and took over the line guarding the left flank. Our Brigade was accordingly transferred to the 22nd Corps, and remained with them for about a fortnight, when we rejoined the Canadians for the last phase.

From Rumaucourt and Saudemont we moved the battery to Sauchy Cauchy on the bank of the Canal. The guns were hidden by a line of fine trees, and accommodation for the Command Post and Wireless was found in some broken down bivouacs left by the Germans. The gun detachments had to rely for shelter on the gun covers. The battery headquarters and detachments off duty, Cook-house, Q.M.S. stores etc. were all located at the old Rumaucourt position which was about a mile distant.

During the fortnight that the battery spent at Sauchy Cauchy, hostile shelling gave us less trouble than usual, though long range guns harassed the pontoon bridge and a girder bridge which the R.E's built across the Canal there.

At first the intention was for the battery to remain silent, but this idea was soon abandoned and a spell of great activity ensued. On some days we fired as many as a thousand rounds. The guns gave signs of breaking down under the strain, and in turn were sent to workshops for overhaul. The men stuck it well and so far as we were concerned the enemy had no rest. Roads, Batteries, Dumps, and Transport—we strafed them collectively and in turn. It became evident that the Germans must retreat from our left and leave the Canal de la Sensee as completely in our hands as was the Canal du Nord. Indeed they seem to have realised this as was shown by the skies being lighted each night by the glare of burning camps and stores which they were unable to take with them.

Between October 10th and November 5th the O.C. went to Brigade as Acting Brigade Commander during Colonel Wilkinson's absence on leave. During this period Major F. D. Field took over the charge of the battery, carrying on with much acceptance the work that fell to our lot. While at Brigade the O.C. carried through a shoot successfully from the roof of Brigade H.Q. From the battery at Sauchy Cauchy the range to the target was 6000 yards and from the Brigade it was 13000 yards. Through a captured German binocular telescope, the Huns could be seen moving on the Bugnicourt Road and the battery was soon ranged. To see men at a distance of 13000 yards and be able to engage them is most unusual, and shows how great an advantage the German artillery had over our's in the quality of their optical instruments.

On October 11th the O.C. visited Cambrai, Cantaing Mill and Marcoing—names fraught with memories of almost exactly a year before.

CHAPTER XIII.

THE PURSUIT.

By 6th October there were rumours of another forward move for the guns. Aeroplane shoots were once again an almost daily diversion, and harassing fire along the Cantin-Douai road kept us busy at night. A struggle was in progress along the Canal, and on 13th October, the village of Aubigny, which had been one of our targets since the Rumaucourt days, changed hands more than once. On 14th October we received orders to move two guns forward to the southern edge of Quesnoy Wood in order to harass the German retreat so confidently anticipated by the Canadians. The move was successfully and expeditiously accomplished in the moonlight, though a low-flying enemy plane held us up for some moments in Oisy le Verger, a village that bore ample evidence of harsh handling by both sides and yet yielded numerous souvenirs. We had an uncomfortable reception at the position, for some twenty 4·2 shells dropped close around us as we laid out the "line", and there were only roughly improvised shelters for the night. Next morning we discovered dugouts, connected with German reserve machine gun posts, in which we could ignore the heavy concentrations to which the Germans subjected us for two days and nights. This was the usual prelude to a retreat and we were not surprised to learn (17th October), that Douai had fallen. During this week particularly thick weather facilitated the enemy's withdrawal, and so little did we know of his doings, that although we had orders to "stand by" about three o'clock on the 17th, we did not open fire.

All was commotion in the evening when the remaining guns were brought up from Sauchy Cauchy and the billets party arrived from Rumaucourt. Billets were selected in Oisy le Verger, but these were not occupied, for the battery had to move back to Rumaucourt in order to get across the Canal de la Sensee. The intention was to cross the Canal at Aubigny, but the R.E.'s had run short of bridging material, and the bridge there could not be repaired. The detachments off duty remained at Rumaucourt, where they were joined later that night by some of the party left at Oisy le Verger who walked back.

The, guns with their on-duty detachments, went north to cross the Canal and made for Cantin, where the night was spent in a concrete factory. We noted the effect of our fire on enemy organizations round the town : we had done as much damage as we hoped. The next day we went on to Fosse St. Roche and the day following to Rœulx.

Our Brigade had been ordered to occupy Auberchicourt, but shortage of water for the horses of the Heavies made Rœulx a more suitable halting place. We were struck in Auberchicourt by the appearance at her door of an old lady who, smiling through the tears that rolled down her cheeks, frantically waved a flag of welcome.

5.

We had a rousing reception at each flag-decorated village, where the inhabitants felt that at last the iron heel of Prussianism was lifted from their necks. We listened to heart-rending tales of bitter oppression and revolting stories of the incredible barbarities of the Germans. Life in occupied France under the Prussian regime is a tale that can never be fully written.

On 22nd October, a position was taken up at the mining village of Haveluy, and the guns came into action once again. The vibration during fire smashed the glass in neighbouring windows and scared the villagers. We were the only Brigade to come into action here.

It was here that Gr. G. H. Fielding displayed the courage of a real hero. He was taken to the 1st Canadian Casualty Clearing Station at Auberchicourt, suffering from a bad cut in the toe caused accidentally by the spade of the gun. While in hospital, he voluntarily yielded 18 ozs of his blood for transfusion into a badly wounded patient. His plucky act unfortunately did not save the man's life, but Gr. Fielding was granted the three week's leave that such deeds of sacrifice demand as much as they deserve.

Ordered forward again we reached Herin on the 24th, and got into action at once.

Here Mr. Huxford joined us, coming from England. He had previously commanded the battery for a few days in July 1917 when we were in Ypres. Despite the many changes in our personnel, a good number remembered his former brief association with the battery.

Rumaucourt was now far in the back areas and it was necessary for the whole battery to be brought together in view of further movements or new developments, for it was evident that the enemy was playing a desperate game with his last cards. It was nearly a day's journey from billets to battery along roads that were uneven at the best, pitted with shell holes in parts, and destroyed by mine explosions at every cross-roads and railway crossing. Travelling by night was dangerous. On 25th October, the remainder of the personnel brought up the stores from Rumaucourt and the battery was at full complement in Herin. We were sorry to leave a place with so many memories grave and gay, but war has little to do with sentiment and we left Rumaucourt to its deep silence. By now the inhabitants will have returned to rebuild and refurnish their quondam homes; our old billets will afford them shelter till the village smiles again.

Our Herin position was in the corner of an orchard by a factory ruined in malice by the retiring enemy. Here we and our sister batteries did much counter-battery work; indeed at this time several Brigades of the Corps H.A. were temporarily resting, and to our Brigade was given the task of engaging most of the Heavy Artillery opposed to us.

Any degree of success in retirement for the enemy depended upon his ability to hold up our advance at Valenciennes for a considerable time, so it was here that he made a stronger resistance than at any point of the whole line from Flanders to the Argonne. He was still going back to the South of us, but to the North he regarded Valenciennes as the hinge to his still open door. This stiffer resistance took the form of heavy street fighting and determined opposition from machine gunners to our infantry, and to us, a recrudescence of enemy shelling to an extent to which we had become unaccustomed. It is probable that some disorganization of his air service saved the batteries of our Brigade from destructive shoots, but it was pretty clear at this time that all our positions were fairly well known to the enemy. Harassing fire, area shoots, and gas shelling worried us considerably.

On the first day our cookhouse was twice hit by 4·2 shells, unfortunately just as tea was being served. We happily had no casualty, but our rations were sadly interfered with.

One or two of the N.C.O's and men were gassed (a gas shell landed at the entrance to the Sergeants' hut) and several were wounded by flying shell splinters. Our worst day was 30th October, when Bdr. E. Evans and Grs. Hood, Slaney, and Williamson were wounded by splinters from a shell which killed the horse they were trying to rescue from a burning barn as they shifted ammunition which was dangerously close. Yet we were fortunate in escaping so lightly, for our guns were seldom allowed to cool. Fortunately two of the cellars of the brewery behind the guns gave adequate protection to the men off duty, and the whole battery was within easy reach of this excellent shelter or of the numerous house cellars.

While still acting as Brigade Commander, our O.C. chancing to visit for the first time an O.P. which had just been established on the top of Fosse du Temple (a big mine slag heap), had such an opportunity of counter-battery work as seldom occurs. With the help of a German binocular telescope, six batteries of artillery were seen in the open, firing, as we learned later, in support of a counter attack on Mont Houy, which was then in our hands and was the key position to the City of Valenciennes. Unfortunately no line existed between this O.P. and our battery, but communication was possible with 195 Siege Battery through 12th Heavy Battery's Exchange. All six were engaged with satisfactory results; three simultaneously by three sections of 195 S.B. and two by 12th H.B.'s 60-pdrs. ranged by Capt. Le Lievre. Casualties were inflicted on three of them and all were driven away in great confusion. The shoot was into the area covered by the 51st (Highland) Division attached to the 22nd Corps on our right.

Two days later the big attack was launched with the object of carrying and passing the Canal and City of Valenciennes. This battle resembled in many respects the Battle of the Canal du Nord, especially in being a sweeping movement from right to left across our front. The main attack started from Mont Houy, a wooded height on the far side of the Canal, and was undertaken by the 22nd Corps. The frontal attack on the city itself across the Canal (undertaken by the Canadians), was a secondary operation, and was dependant upon the success of the outflanking advance from Mt. Houy. In this battle a very heavy barrage was put down by the 6-inch Howitzers of several Brigades—an unusual feature, for the barrage had latterly been left to the Field Artillery. The Brigade of heavy artillery engaged in Counter-battery work was at a disadvantage which called for special methods. The locations of hostile batteries were not well known, and at this time were changing daily. It was therefore impossible to work out a prearranged counter-battery programme, and batteries had to be engaged as they were seen to become active. At zero hour C.-B. batteries engaged many batteries which were supposed to be active, the artillery 'planes, of which many were in use, signalled the numbers of any of these seen to be inactive, sending at the same time locations of others which could be seen firing. Our guns were continually switched off batteries which became inactive on to these fresh targets, so as to leave no active battery unengaged. This plan seemed to work very well, and during the day our Brigade dealt with 59 NF calls, many of which were fired on by more than one battery. We ourselves expended fourteen hundred and two rounds in this way.

Valenciennes fell into our hands and next day we moved forward to St. Waast la Haut, where, owing to our proximity to the main road, we were shelled a good deal that night. Here on the morning of the 3rd we opened on our S.O.S. lines to stop a threatened counter-attack. On the following day we passed forward through the fine city of Valenciennes, noting the complete destruction of the Canal Bridges and railway station, though we found the town itself practically unharmed. We were billeted that night with civilians at Marly, where Major Delap rejoined us, the Brigade Commander having come back from leave. Two guns were brought into action in the open near Estreux. The bad condition of the roads, no less than the craters left by the Huns, gave infinite trouble and caused much delay. The roads in this part of the country were made with a paved centre only, and any vehicle which failed to keep on this was usually ditched more or less hopelessly.

These were wet days and in this position little cover could be found for the men on the guns, who had to make the best of things in tents, while the opposition offered by "King Mud" to our advance reminded some of us of the 1916 winter on the Somme. On both the 5th and 6th we took part in early morning bombardments in support of further advances by the Canadian Infantry.

Meanwhile the other four guns went forward to Rombies and got into action at Rouge Haie Farm, just short of that village. They also took part in an attack which was made on the morning of the 6th November on strong German rearguards. We had now to collect the two guns which remained at the Estreux position, and to get these out we made use of a "Caterpillar", thoughtfully supplied by Corps H.A. for the rescue of guns which might happen to get into difficulties. This useful but ungainly creature, whose kind is popularly supposed to revel in deep mud, breathed its last soon after pulling our guns on to the road, and we left it stuck in about three feet of mud, its driver regarding it pessimistically.

The next day all the guns were parked in Rombies village, and officers and men found billets there. The war seemed to have died away, and it was on this day that we heard the first reliable rumours of a possible outbreak of peace. These were in the form of instructions regulating our behaviour should we chance to meet a Hun with a white flag, a not unnecessary precaution.

On 8th November orders were received for a further advance, and on the 9th we crossed the Belgian frontier and pulled out on to the main Mons Road. That day of seeming peace was evidently the prelude to a big German retirement, and the question was whether they were going to make a stand on the Mons-Maubeuge line, or go right back to Charleroi. This uncertainty caused some delay in the issue of orders, and it was not until the late afternoon that we parked on the main road just short of Boussu. Here we had tea, and experienced the unwelcome attentions of a German 4·2 gun at long range. Had we only known it we should have rejoiced to think that we were never to be under shell-fire again. By evening we got orders to go on into Boussu and billet there. This we did with some success, finding quarters for officers and men at a large Cafe in the Square. We had a boisterous welcome from the inhabitants, and indeed all that day civilians had done their best to impede us with gifts and rejoicings as much as by their inveterate habit of wheeling a barrow-full of furniture across the road in front of any lorry they could see. Bedtime came at last and everyone looked forward to a well earned rest; but the gods willed otherwise. At 1.50 a.m. on the 10th a despatch rider burst his way into the O.C's bedroom and handed in two messages, one to the effect that the Kaiser had abdicated, and the other that the battery would "proceed forthwith", take up position near a certain mining village, a suburb of Mons, and be in action by 6 a.m. with four hundred rounds of ammunition and a telephone line laid to Corps H.A. This was a bitter blow—and looked very much like an impossibility as well; we knew from previous experience that nearly every cross-road was blown up, and the way lay through suburbs, mining villages, pitheads, railways, and all the obstacles of an industrial neighbourhood; the night was pitch dark and the map unreliable. However, 6 a.m. on the 10th saw us at our position, with ammunition in readiness and communication established by runner. We should have had a line if the position of Corps H.A. had been correctly given. As it was Mr. Yardley and his Signallers got their line through soon after.

Orders to open fire were not immediately received and, pending their arrival, the remainder of our stores and ammunition was brought up, and an O.P. was established in a Cafe at the cross roads, where we were received with the greatest delight.   A big crowd of civilians gradually collected round the guns, and were only persuaded to depart when it was explained to them that their presence would probably give away the Battery and attract a shower of high explosive. The effect of this warning was immediate.

Meanwhile the usual billeting parties were meeting with un-expected success. From the houses which they visited, the inhabitants on seeing them, rushed with joyful shouts, and begging them to enter, placed all at their disposal. We were the first British who had been seen in this locality since those dreadful days in 1914, when the strength of the Allies had been insufficient to stem the invasion of the enemy, and the welcome they gave us was genuine and delightful.   At every house coffee was prepared, and they thought it an honour to entertain us.

A few targets came through, principally hostile batteries in the outskirts of Mons, and the Hun had not entirely thrown up the sponge as was evidenced by occasional shell bursts among the fosses in front of us. It is sad to recall that an officer of a battery close on our right was killed an hour or two before the cessation of hostilities.

That same afternoon (10th November), orders were received at

3.55 that at 4 o'clock we were to open in a rolling barrage with instantaneous fuses east of the town of Mons. This, had we but known it, was the last action in which we were to take part. It was also the shortest notice we had ever received of an operation of this character and called for some high speed thinking by B.C.A's Trotter and Miller. "C" gun fired the last round in this barrage, our last shot and the last barrage of the war.

The Major, who was at an O.P. on a fosse in front of the Battery, describes this, the last scene in the great drama of war, as most picturesque. Behind, sunset and a sea of mist pierced by the tops of innumerable fosses and stippled with the incessant flicker of a thousand guns. In front, Mons, at once the start and finish of our war, lit by the glare of burning houses and encircled by the smoke of British shells. We and the Belgians who accompanied us could not but feel some triumph at this fitting climax.

The last Germans were driven out of Mons at 2 a.m. on the morning of the 11th.

CHAPTER XIV.

THE ARMISTICE.

" Priority. All Batteries.

G121. 11:11:18. AAA.

Hostilities will cease at 1100 hours on Nov. 11. Troops will stand fast on line reached at that hour which will be reported to Corps H.Q. Defensive precautions will be maintained. There will be no intercourse with the enemy. Further instructions will follow. Addressed all concerned. C.C.H.A."

" M 4.

L 775 11:11:18. AAA.

Further to wire G121 re cessation of hostilities. On no account is any firing to take place after 1100 hours to-day AAA. Acknowledge. M 0900 hours."

These were the messages we received on the morning of the 11th November. This was the news which was to change the whole tenor of our existence. In London, we believe, it was received with great excitement; buses were overturned, captured trophies were destroyed and relief and pleasure manifested in many strange ways. To us, though expected, the news came as a surprise. The situation which we had come to regard almost as an impossibility—Incredible! and yet—so we took it, soberly, and verging on disbelief; the thing was really our charter of release, and realization of it came with time.

That afternoon some of us were privileged to witness a moving ceremony—the British handing over the town of Mons to the Burgomaster. Here were bands in plenty and a smart parade. The people of Mons, delirious with joy, had decked their town with Belgian and Allied flags and gave us a great welcome. But to one who watched, the most moving feature was to hear a British band playing " Tipperary" in the streets of Mons. Long years had passed of bitter struggle since that air had echoed in those streets before.

We spent the ensuing fortnight with our kind friends at Flenu. With them we shared our rations and exchanged views, the conversations being brilliant examples of facial contortion and manual dexterity, relieved by interjaculatory nothings, half a dozen cosmopolitan words, and a " compree". Yet we felt we had conveyed our meaning to them, though we might not be fully satisfied in our own minds that we had quite understood theirs.

In the yard of the Charbonnage the guns were parked and cleaned. At Flenu the battery was photographed. Unfortunately the day was very misty and the photograph though good was not unexceptionable. Our early departure to Germany led to the breakdown of negotiations for the purchase of copies, but when we reached our destination on the Rhine the O.C. photographed us as a battery and by sections. All these pictures proved excellent and are our best souvenirs of "303".

By this time we knew we had been selected to take part in the advance to the Rhine, and passing through the usual period of rumour and parade, got our twelve hour notice late in the evening of 26th November. We may pass over the little worries incidental to our start, and the real sorrow of the villagers at our departure early next day. We were warned that we might have to parade for an inspection " en route", and speculated as to the possibility of a march past King Albert of Belgium who was making his official entry into Mons that day. We rode through Frameries and then round the beautiful avenue that encircles the historic town of Mons. The inspection did not take place.

We pushed on by Binche to Morlanwelz (or Mariemont as the Francophile inhabitants prefer to call it) which we reached about 5.30 p.m. The journey had been slow and cold owing to the congested roads, but we were billeted with a willing people and spent an enjoyable evening in the town.

Next day after an early start, we travelled through a number of villages to Velaine-sur-Sambre, where we arrived in pouring rain and were accommodated in commodious school-rooms. This village was the scene of one of those frightful massacres which earned for Germany the detestation of the whole world. In the opening days of the war, four hundred civilians were shot down with machine guns in their Market Square. The people showed a sort of apathetic interest in our progress, but there was no enthusiasm or excitement over our column and no welcome such as we had received the previous day. All the villages were decorated, but we missed the hearty greetings displayed at Morlanwelz, where "Welcome to the brave Englische soldiers" showed that the hearts of the inhabitants were at least more liberal than their knowledge of our language.

We mounted our lorries and moved out from Velaine early on the 29th. As we passed through Onoz-Spy the character of the scenery changed abruptly, monotonous flat ground giving place to' diversified hill country. All along we continued to pass derelict German material and at the entrance of the village of Temploix, the effigy of a German soldier fully equipped and hung by the neck from a telegraph pole showed what some of us thought was the real feeling of the people, others the grim humour of the Canadians. We traversed Belgrade and approached Namur itself, reaching the famous city at the confluence of the Sambre and Meuse shortly after 9 a.m. Moving slowly through the town, we were struck with the wealth of flags displayed, the French, American, Italian, and British adding a note of brightness to the more sombre and preponderating Belgian banner. We had an excellent view of the historic Citadel as we crossed the bridge towards Jambes, where we were to rest. Our lorries took us nearly a mile up the hill beyond the suburb, a point from which we had an unobstructed panoramic view over the city. We marched back to the "Ecole des Soeurs de la Providence", where once again we succeeded German troops in quarters. The Sisters were particularly kind to us and strove in every way to make us comfortable. Here we remained till December 1st, visiting the city in the afternoons and evenings. The Citadel, Cathedral, and other places interested us, and the Censoring Officers bear witness that many post cards were sent off. Here also we saw many returned Allied prisoners, soldiers and civilians, who were brought up the river daily by steamboat. Some of the soldiers were in a famishing condition and insufficiently clothed.

On the evening before we left, the inhabitants took it into their heads to wreck the houses of some of their fellow-townspeople whom they had suspected of pro-German leanings. It was an extraordinary sight to see them throwing wardrobes from the top-floor windows into the street.

From Namur onwards, we were side-tracked to most uninteresting villages, approached for the most part by equally uninteresting roads. Of these halting places on the great journey, it is sufficient to name Sin Sin to recall to each one's memory what every one thought; as a contrast we think pleasantly of the lovely valley approach to Amonines. Everyone was charmed with the road thither and above all by the magnificent situation of the little town of Laroche, a veritable gem of the Ardennes. At Amonines the people, poor though they were, displayed very great kindness towards us and insisted on our sharing with them their homely fare. Our next stop was almost on the German-Luxembourg-Belgian frontier. We found billets in the village of Gouvy, lately an important German railway concentration point. A visit to the village will, however, dispel the visions conjured up by those at home who received picturesque postcards of this place. Here we remained from December 5th till December 9th, waiting until arrangements were completed for our crossing the frontier.

At 7.45 a.m. on the 9th December, we crossed into Germany without either ceremony or emotion. We noted in crossing the destroyed German frontier post, symbolic of her present position. The first village at which we rested was Valender, prettily situated in a valley. Here we spent the night before proceeding next morning past several fine fir plantations, and at least one fine beech wood by Bollingen to Ramscheid. The next day we viewed some magnificent valley scenery as we left the Eifel high ground to descend on to the Rhine plain. Passing through prosperous Euskirchen we reached the town of Rheinbach where we billeted for the night.

The following day (12th December) it had been arranged that we, with 195 Siege Battery and the two 6-inch Howitzer Batteries of the 16th Brigade · R.G.A., should take up position in support of our infantry crossing the Rhine. Leaving Rheinbach at 9 a.m., a short two hours run brought us to the outskirts of Bonn. Here with 303 Siege Battery leading, the column formed up for the entry into the town. With the Colonel at the head, this lumbering cavalcade rumbled through the streets and, reaching the banks of the Rhine, took up position there, we and 195 Siege Battery on the north of the bridge and the other two batteries on the south side of it.

The Heavy Artillery destined for Cologne were a day behind us; thus our position at the head of the Brigade secured for us the distinction of being the first battery of Heavy Artillery to reach the Rhine.

We will end our story with an extract from a Special Order of the Day dated 12th December 1918 :—

> "The deployment of the British Batteries of Heavy Artillery on the banks of the Rhine, to cover the advance of the 2nd Canadian Division crossing the river, will long be remembered by all who were privileged to take part."

"THERE IS A BATTERY OF HOWITZERS ON THE RHINE BANK."

What are you thinking of—silent Gun?
I think of the work that is nearly done.
I think of a France that was turned to Hell.
I think of the Gunners who served me well.
Up to my axles in slime and mud,
With my breech block smothered in brave men's blood,
Re-set and painted—tested and true,
I am ready to start on my work anew.

What do you see, you painted thing?
I see the throne of a fugitive King.
Freedom's troops on a country side,
Where once were the Castles of Crime and Pride.
A River, the boast of a race accursed,
Who tried their best to do their worst.
Proudly I look at my mates in line,
The real indisputable "Wacht am Rhein."

What do you hear, you great dumb beast?
I hear a rumour from West to East,
Of an Army to hold what we dearly bought,
To keep the position for which we fought.
The south wind whispers from far Mayence,
The river is held in the name of France.
And the ripples sing from the racing tide,
America stands at your right hand side.

Why do you laugh, you great grim Gun?
I laugh to think of the frolic and fun,
When back in old England around my Wheels,
Children will gambol with joyful squeals,
Lovers in couples will sit on my trail,
And my ears will be cheered with the old, old tale.
Be sure there'll be plenty of laughter and fun,
When the war is past and my work is done.

No. 1 GUN IN POSITION AT BONN, DECEMBER 12th. 1918.

This was the first gun of the British Heavy Artillery to reach the Rhine.

CHAPTER XV.

"O.P.'s"

No history of the battery would be complete without a short chapter on "O.P.'s", though interest in the subject is confined chiefly to Officers, observers, and signallers. For them, certain phrases, "Q1d", "Lone Tree", "Datum House", "Station Avenue", will always bring back memories not altogether unpleasant. For there were many compensations, such as hearing Gunner Jackson explaining to a group of admiring Infantry exactly how to tell the bearing of hostile shelling or testing the results of the signallers' "candle-cookery".

In spite of many exciting walks to, and uncomfortable moments at our numerous O.P.'s, we were fortunate in escaping with only one O.P. casualty (Lieut. Bloye slightly wounded at Saudemont) during our 19 months active service; though many a linesman had an unrecorded narrow squeak when on his thankless and unenviable job of looking for a new break in the cable.

To deal with the subject chronologically:—

Our first and undoubted "cushiest" O.P. was in one of the tunnels which form the rabbit warren that once was Kemmel Hill. It was approached by a pleasant country walk ending in the wooded slope leading up to the Hill which was never shelled in those days. Once ensconced in the eastern end of the tunnel one had a good view of and beyond the Messines-Wytchaete Ridge, but was still 2000 yards from the front line and "safer than a house". From here we had good observation of the Dammstrasse and other targets on which we fired hundreds of rounds per gun, in preparation for the Messines battle of June 7th.

During the first part of our stay in Ypres we had no regular O.P. For the occasional purposes of registration, "Haslar House" in St. Jean was used; the ruins of a "Chateau" filled with concrete, from which the original brickwork was gradually knocked away, ultimately leaving the concrete kernel exposed.

After July 31st Bossaert's Farm, or the remaining wall of the farm, was manned on two occasions, but its exposed situation in the support line, then in the process of being dug, rendered it untenable. These never-to-be-forgotten days immediately after the partially successful attack of July 31st supplied at least two officers with all the experience they could desire of Flanders mud. After this we manned an O.P. in "Liverpool Trench" whence we frequently registered on "Wurst Farm" and saw the beginning of the numerous local attacks on the "pill-boxes" which defended the Passchendaele ridge.

When we moved south for the winter, we were fortunate in finding an O.P. which, after a little attention, was quite in keeping with our sumptuous billets and the peace front. It was situated in High Wood, whence we had a fine view of Havrincourt, Flesquieres and Ribecourt—all names famous in later battery history. Here we first knew the joys of a dug-out—and by the irony of fate had only one shell within a hundred yards during the two months that we manned it. These were, indeed, very quiet times, when the only excitement was provided by the nightly struggle at the entrance to the dug-out between the rats and a particularly pugnacious weasel. If one wanted a pleasant walk in those days, there was always the front line to visit, where the trenches held by the 36th (Ulster) Division were perfect works of art. In a sap in front of one of these trenches was an R.F.A. O.P. of which we made use on occasions; in particular, one day we had a very successful little strafe on " Peter", the T.M. in "Boggart's Hole", which had been annoying the Infantry at night.

During the troublous times that followed, when the Battery was in position between Flesquières and Ribecourt, a wrecked "tank" proved a very handy O.P., being less than 50 yards from the Officers' Mess—until hostile shelling made it too uncomfortable. We then moved to "Kaiser Trench" amid the sad remains of many other derelict tanks, where our chief recollection is of ice, snow and cold feet.

Early in January it was discovered that a fine view was obtainable from the second floor of Flesquières Chateau. Accordingly we took up our position in what had been the nursery—the wall-paper illustrated incidents in the adventures of John Gilpin, and the floor was strewn with old exercise books! The ground sloped gradually upwards to Bourlon Wood and Fontaine-notre-Dame, and many were the working parties "dispersed with casualties" by our guns. On one occasion the General in command of the H.A.—apparently his first visit to an O.P.!—was delighted at the sight of a Hun "spitting on his hands" and later hurriedly took cover. One of the chief attractions of this spot was the canteen in the cellar, where cocoa or soup was generally to be had for the asking. During the nights we moved to dug-outs on the Ribecourt road, which was a fortunate arrangement, as the nursery was twice hit at night, rendering it slightly draughty though not entirely uninhabitable.

After the retreat at the end of March, our first O.P. was in an orchard near Auchonvillers—familiarly known as "Eight-inch Villas". The advantages of this place were nil. Among its disadvantages we may note: there was but a very poor field of view, very little cover and five yards away was an obvious enemy registration-point. The inevitable—a direct hit from a 5·9—happened on April 23rd, when the O.P. party had fortunately withdrawn to the shelter of a neighbouring cellar. This undesirable spot was manned only by day, but several times we had orders to be there by 3 a.m., an enemy attack being expected. Usually these days turned out to be particularly dull and uneventful. On April 5th an attack actually did take place, and Lieut. Archer distinguished himself by three times walking through a 5·9 barrage in order to get a message through.

During the early part of April, before we had fully settled down to trench warfare again, we made several special excursions to a flank O.P. on the Mesnil Ridge to the right of Auchonvillers. From here on the 3rd we spotted four hostile batteries in action in the open. Two of these proved to be within range, and in spite of the

8000 yards of telephone wire which provided communication across shelled areas, were most successfully engaged and finally silenced to the delight of the Infantry holding the Ridge, who had been considerably worried by the activities of these very batteries.

After April 23rd we established ourselves in a "pill-box" in front of Colincamps, known as "Apple-tree O.P." This we manned day and night for three months, accompanied by a representative of the 12th Heavy Battery; and it was here that O.P. work reached its highest standard. Communication was almost entirely by buried cable and supplemented by Lucas lamps; we were supplied with S.O.S. rockets, rifles, log-books, and visibility maps. The pill-box itself was of reinforced concrete, and was built in 1916 as an advanced Headquarters for some Infantry Brigade in the opening stages of the Battle of the Somme; but to add to our comfort towards the end of May, we re-opened a large dug-out with three entrances, which provided our signallers (and others) with good cover. Curiously enough on the first day that this dug-out was used, a 4·2 shell fell in one entrance, entirely smashing up the "bivvy" in which the signallers had hitherto been installed.

During the whole of this period those in authority were daily expecting a hostile attack which never came off. Indeed our impression was that the enemy were expecting an attack from us; the Staff on each side trembling for fear of the other.

But Appletrees O.P. will always be remembered for the amount of successful "liaison" work carried on. First of all of course there was 12th Heavies; the log-book bore witness to the friendly rivalry existing between us, the delight with which we usually recorded whenever "12" had a successful registration, and above all the famous day when one of their shells managed to score a direct hit on the "lone-tree"! Undoubtedly our most interesting acquaintances were the New Zealand Field-gunners, who, both officers and men wittingly or unwittingly, did much to vary the monotony of our existence. It was a noteworthy sight to see four or five stalwart "Diggers", clad only in shorts and boots, with their bodies as bronzed as Red Indians, playing cricket about a thousand yards from our front line. Another incident is worth recording; one night the Corps on our right had a trench-raid, and having omitted to warn the Corps on our left, the latter got the "wind up", and started sending up the S.O.S.; the results were a pretty fire-work display in which, as was his wont, the Boche joined, and later plenty of noise on both flanks. This noise must have roused the New Zealander on duty from his slumbers, for in spite of the calm prevailing on our immediate front, he fired off one of his S.O.S. rockets and reported the matter to his officer. The latter, who had long wanted the chance to let off some rockets, fired another, other sentries in the neighbourhood joined in, and the Boche received a pretty strong dose of "iron-rations" before it was discovered that a false alarm had been given.

During July we had many unusual visitors, including several "balloonatics" from No. 44 Balloon Section, Padre Newell, Lieut. Oliver, A.S.C., the O.C. Fourth Corps Siege Park—and the Assistant Orderly Officer of our Brigade. The last named is said to have arrived at the O.P. in a fainting condition, but recovered in the dug-out with the assistance of Lieut. Johnson's flask. Our most frequent visitor was Col. Murray, whose almost daily appearance in the trenches gained him a lasting popularity among our New Zealand friends. One of his noteworthy amusements was to motor-cycle back to Brigade H.Q. via the Sugary and Colincamps. Another incident worth recording was the first arrival of Capt. Grayson at Apple-trees, when he was put under arrest on suspicion of being a German spy by the alert officer of 121 Heavy Battery on duty, presumably because he had absent-mindedly appeared in a British Warm with two "pips" on one shoulder and one on the other. And we must not forget to mention "Heinrich", the enterprising German who used to sit out in No-man's land invisible from our trenches but clearly seen from our O.P.'s. The N.Z.F.A. refused to disturb him, but later on a 4·5 Howitzer Battery of the 42nd Division were unkind enough to drop a few rounds unpleasantly near him, and we did not see him again.

After we pulled out from Beaussart on July 30th, we were almost continually on the move until the cessation of hostilities on November 11th. The O.P.'s manned during this period were numerous, but at none of them did we stay long enough to make them worthy of more than passing mention. We remember Rosières Church Tower during August; the sand pit near Saudemont (formerly a Boche reserve O.P.), during September, where Lieut. Bloye was wounded on the 24th; Oisy-le-Verger and Quesnoy Wood during the first part of October; and lastly numerous fosses during our final advance. From one of these Major Delap successfully engaged four hostile batteries with their teams of horses standing by ready to pull out, firing in support of a counter-attack on the Corps on our right, (this counter-attack was a forlorn hope directed against Mont Houy, a key position south of Valenciennes). From another near Flénu, we watched our rolling barrage on the afternoon of November 10th, our final action before the Armistice put an end to hostilities.

In conclusion, we should not forget to mention our two observers, Bombardier Hancocks and Gunner Jackson, who, during the last fourteen months of the Battery's active service, shared with the Observing Officer the perils, joys, boredom and excitement of "Oh-pipping".

CHAPTER XVI.

SIGNALS, WIRELESS AND LEWIS GUNS.

It has been difficult in compiling the history of the Battery to deal fittingly with the Signallers and the work they have done. The laying and maintenance of a system of telephonic communication is an essential and important part of the work of a Siege Battery in action. As soon as a position has been selected, a line is at once laid to Brigade H.Q., and another to the O.P. Other lines will be wanted running to the Wireless, Balloon, Officers' Mess, Billets, possibly detached sections, etc. This system necessitates the use of an Exchange at which the different stations can be connected. In addition to this, provision has to be made for visual signalling from most of these points in the event of the line breaking down. Reliefs of Signallers are arranged for running the stations, some permanently, others as required, and linesmen are kept ready to examine and repair any lines which may get broken. It is not intended to describe the whole work of the Signal Section, but we may mention the need for raising a telephone line on poles when crossing roads and tracks, for digging it in below the surface in areas specially exposed to shell fire, for "tapping in" stations on long lines to facilitate the location of a break, and the provision of alternate routes to provide against hostile shelling.

The Signaller's duties are necessarily performed in rather isolated positions. While gunners in their sometimes dangerous duties are supported by the presence of their fellows, the signallers as a rule work in pairs far from help, each man dependent only on his comrade for support. This sometimes calls for qualities of initiative and determination of a high order. Some of the advantages of their calling are that they share with officers and observers the interest of seeing shoots from the O.P. end of the line and that, except in times of special stress, they have less disturbed nights than the gunners.

During our early days in France, the signallers were under the charge of Cpl. Moor, assisted by Cpl. Sharp. On Cpl. Moor's promotion to Sergeant, he left the Signallers for a time for duty on the guns, and Cpl. Sharp took over from him and continued until his unfortunate death at Trescault in the First Battle of Cambrai. Sergt. Moor again took the Signallers on until he went on leave, when his place was taken by Cpl. Worthington, who was posted to us from the Base. He was a very efficient Signalling N.C.O. and was promoted to Sergeant just before his removal to hospital suffering from Influenza at Beaussart in June 1918. Sergt. Moor's third and last spell with the Signallers was from September 1918 to the Rhine. In spite of his periods at other duty he has always kept in touch with the Signallers, and their success throughout has been largely due to his skilful supervision.

Among other N.C.O's to be mentioned are Bdrs. Goldsmith, Nelson, Sweetingham, Mottershead, Veitch, Taffs and Brooksbank. Of the Signallers we recall Signallers Buchan (unfortunately killed in another Battery after he left us), Matheson (killed at Ribecourt), and Warner (wounded at Ribecourt), and we must not forget Signaller Stott the gramophone mender, and "The Kids" Slaughter and Booker, so difficult to fit from Army stock sizes.

Lieut. Bloye was the officer longest in charge of the Signal Section, August 1917 to September 1918. He did his best to enlist the sympathies of the O.C. on their behalf! When he was wounded at Saudemont on 14th September 1918, Lieut. Yardley took over his duties with characteristic energy. Previous Signalling Officers were Lieuts. Silverton and Ainscough.

An interesting adjunct to the Signal Sub-section was the Battery Wireless. This is normally manned by two Second Air Mechanics from the R.A.F., which was sometimes the case with us, but we were fortunate in having the assistance of a Battery Signaller who had been trained in Wireless—Signaller Ruff. 1st A/M Wakeley was with us throughout the whole of our War Service and carried out his duties most admirably. The calls he missed could probably be numbered on the fingers of one hand, and he sometimes picked up messages not intended for him, notably at "Hell-Fire Corner", where, by intercepting a German message, he was able to warn the Battery that the Hun was about to open fire on them. He, with Signaller Ruff, had many an adventure. The wireless poles and aerials, damaged by splinters, would be repaired amongst more splinters. At Herin where the wireless was being manned by 2 A/M Hopgood and Signaller Ruff, a shell burst in the roof of the wireless room but without damaging the instrument or frightening the operators.

Another sideline run by the Battery was Lieut. Bloye's Lewis Gun Detachment, consisting of Signallers, B.C.A's, Observers, Spotters, and Officers' Servants. The guns were sited for ground and anti-aircraft work. Air targets were plentiful. We do not remember how many planes were brought down, but a great number of rounds were fired; when they did miss an aeroplane, it was always because "the gun jammed". Captain Grayson's anti-aircraft enthusiasm with the Officers' Lewis Gun at Beaussart did not always meet with the success it deserved, and we fear that the O.C. with his rifle at Ribecourt had not many planes to his credit. The Lewis Gun class will recall the artistic diagrams in the instruction hut at Beaussart. How many remember the difference between a "Camel" and a "Gotha" now?

APPENDIX.

List of Officers

	Joined.	Left.	Remarks.
Castle, 2nd Lieut. S. B.	5 12 16	22 6 17	Wounded.
Landale, 2nd Lieut. A. R. ...	18 12 16	27 7 17	Gassed. Accidentally injured 7 ʋ 17.
Silverton, 2nd Lieut. E. G....	31 12 16		Killed, 26 7 17.
Ledward, Lieut. C. H.	1 1 17		Rhine, December, 1918.
Saidler, Capt. W. T.	17 2 17	16 7 17	To R.F.C.
Lockhart, Major H. W..........	29 3 17	15 7 17	To 51 H.A.G.
Ruffel, 2nd Lieut. W. G.	23 4 17	25 6 17	Wounded.
Green, Laeut. J. N.	8 7 17	29 5 18	To 484 S.B.
Huxford, Actg. Major E. H., M.C.	19 7 17	22 7 17	Gassed. Rejoined as Lieut. 23 10 18. Rhine December, 1918.
Grieg, 2nd Lieut. S. W.........	21 7 17	26 7 17	Wounded.
Steward, Capt. A. T.	26 7 17	14 8 17	Gassed.
Ainscough, 2nd Lieut. T. ...	4 8 17		Killed, 25 1 18.
Guttery, 2nd Lieut. N. A. ...	4 8 17	28 9 17	Accidentally injured.
Bloye, 2nd Lieut. W.	25 8 17	14 9 18	Wounded, 2 9 18 and 14 9 18.
Bennett, Capt. W. D.	26 8 17	6 4 18	To 81 S.B.
Delap, Major J. O. K., D.S.O.	3 9 17		Rhine, December, 1918.
Bleese, 2nd Lieut. J.	12 9 17	9 3 18	
Hoy, 2nd Lieut. A. Y.	14 9 17	26 10 17	To 184 S.B.
Smith, 2nd Lieut. G. A.	11 10 17	24 6 18	To 29th Brigade, R.G.A.
Farrall, 2nd Lieut. S. A. R.	19 10 17	26 10 17	To XVII. Corps, H.A.
Gridley, 2nd Lieut. R. W. ...	22 10 17	26 10 17	To XVII. Corps, H.A.
Dobb, 2nd Lt. W. C. N. F.	9 11 17	11 11 17	Attached ʀ.F.C. as A.O.
Yardley, Lieut. B. W.	9 11 17		Rhine, December, 1918.
Johnson, Lieut. S., M.C.	20 12 17		Killed, 24 9 18.
Archer, 2nd Lieut. E. L.	29 1 18	2 9 18	Wounded.
Grayson, Capt. J. R.	7 4 18		Rhine, December, 1918.
Burroughs, Lieut. G. H.	24 5 18		Rhine, December, 1918.
Sunderland, 2nd Lieut. J. E.	24 5 18		Rhine, December, 1918.
Mockridge, Lieut. A. H.	26 9 18		Rhine, December, 1918.
Oliver, Lieut. S., R.A.ʂ.C. ...	6 9 17		Rhine, December, 1918.

Warrant Officers, Non-Commissioned Officers & Gunners.

Name and Final Rank in Battery.	Date Posted to Battery.	Remarks.
Aitken, Gnr. R.	8 4 18	Rhine, December, 1918.
Albone, Gnr. F. P.	21 9 17	Wounded, 27 9 17.
Alderson, Gnr. J.	29 1 17	Rhine, December, 1918.
Alexander, Gnr. D. D.	29 1 17	Wounded, 23 6 17. To England, 19 7 17.
Allen, Gnr. G.	8 7 17	From 371st S.B. Gassed, 14 7 17. To England, 29 7 17.
Allsopp, Gnr. A.	9 7 18	Rhine, December, 1918.
Allsopp, Gnr. W.	20 11 16	Wounded, 1 6 17. To Base, 11 6 17.
Andrew, Gnr. J. B.	26 7 17	From 5th Army pool. To Base, 13 8 17, sick.
Andrew, Gnr. J. S.	9 7 18	In hospital, 12 12 18.
Annett, Gnr. F. D.	8 7 17	From 371st S.B. Gassed, 14 7 17. To England, 2 8 17.
Atkinson, Gnr. F. P.	4 2 18	Rhine, December, 1918.
Atkinson, Gnr. H.	9 7 18	Rhine, December, 1918.
Bailey, Gnr. W. E.	29 1 17	Wounded, 7 8 17.
Baker, Gnr. H.	7 12 16	Gassed, 14 7 17. To England, 8 8 17.
Ball, Gnr. F. E.	9 7 18	Rhine, December, 1918.

6.

Name and Final Rank in Battery.	Date Posted to Battery.		Remarks.
Ball, Gnr. J. R. K.	9	7 18	Rhine, December, 1918.
Ball, Gnr. J. W.	15	7 18	To Base, 19 11 18, sick.
Ball, Gnr. W. G.	25	2 17	Gassed, 14 7 17. To Base, 2 12 17.
Ball, Cpl. W. R.	8	7 17	From 371st S.B. Wounded 24 7 17. To England, 6 9 17.
Barber, Gnr. B.	25	5 18	Rhine, December, 1918.
Barber, Gnr. W. A.	9	7 18	Rhine, December, 1918.
Barlow, Gnr. W.	14	6 17	To England, sick, 27 10 17.
Barnett, Gnr. J. C.	8	7 17	From 371st S.B. Gassed, 14 7 17. To England, 6 8 17.
Barnfield, Gnr. A. H.	21	9 17	Rhine, December, 1918.
Barnie, Gnr. W. M.	4	2 18	Rhine, December, 1918.
Barrett, Gnr. F.	22	1 18	To Base, sick, 6 7 18.
Bates, Gnr. W. C.	29	1 17	Gassed, 14 7 17.
Bath, Gnr. W. J.	2	12 16	Wounded, 7 8 17. To England, sick, 22 9 18.
Beardsworth, Gnr. J. B. ...	31	8 17	Rhine, December, 1918.
Beecroft, Gnr. J. H.	29	1 17	Wounded, 19 6 17. Accidentally injured, 21 6 18
Bennett, Gnr. T. J.	8	7 17	From 371st S.B. Wounded, 28 7 17. To Base, 17 8 17.
Bennett, Cpl. W. G.	6	12 16	Rhine, December, 1918.
Beresford, Gnr. F.	8	7 17	From 371st S.B. Gassed, 14 7 17. To England, 24 7 17.
Berry, Gnr. G.	8	7 17	From 371st S.B. Killed in action, 11 7 17.
Betts, Actg. Bmdr. L. G....	8	7 17	From 371st S.B. Gassed, 13 7 17. To England, 4 8 17.
Beveridge, Cpl. J.	16	9 17	From 9th S.B. Rejoined 9th S.B. 12 10 17.
Beveridge, Gnr. W.	25	2 17	Wounded, 1 1 18. To England, 14 1 18.
Biffin, Cpl. A.	8	7 17	From 371st S.B. Gassed, 14 7 17. To England, sick, 22 10 17.
Bingham, Gnr. C.	20	11 16	Wounded, 7 7 17. To England, 26 7 17.
Birch, Gnr. W. W.	8	7 17	From 371st S.B. Gassed, 14 7 17. To England, sick, 14 7 18.
Bird, Cpl. J. F.	17	2 17	Gassed, 14 7 17. To Base, 24 8 17. Reposted to battery, 15 9 17. To England, for posting to Cadet unit, 13 2 18.
Birrell, Actg. Bmdr. J. L.	20	11 17	Rhine, December, 1918.
Bishop, Gnr. E. C. G.	8	4 18	To England, sick, 10 5 18.
Blair, Gnr. G.	4	12 16	To Base, sick, 27 9 17.
Blake, Sergt. A. E.	8	7 17	From 371st S.B. Wounded, 11 7 17. Died, 8 8 17.
Blatchford, Gnr. F. H......	11	5 18	To England, sick, 7 7 18.
Bleakley, Smith Gnr. H. ...	13	3 17	Gassed, 17 7 17. To England, 8 8 17.
Booker, Gnr. E.	3	8 17	To Base, sick, 29 8 17.
Booth, Gnr. F.	9	7 18	Rhine, December, 1918.
Booth, Gnr. T., M.M.	9	7 18	Rhine, December, 1918.
Boswell, Cpl. A. S.	10	8 17	From 62nd H.A.G. Wounded, 18 8 17. To England, 30 8 17.
Bowes, Actg. Bmdr. A.	25	11 16	Wounded, 11 7 17. To England, 16 7 17.
Boylan, Gnr. L.	2	12 16	To Base, 14 7 17, sick.
Bramwell, Gnr. A.	14	6 17	Wounded, 7 7 17. Died from wounds, 14 7 17.
Brassett, B.S.M. G.W.	5	2 18	Wounded, 6 4 18. To England, 11 4 18.
Breary, Gnr. H.	8	7 17	From 371st S.B. Gassed, 14 7 17. To England, 8 8 17.
Brewer, Cpl. J. H.	25	11 16	Wounded, 7 8 17. Wounded, 15 8 17. To Base, 4 9 17. Reported from Base 13 9 17. To Home Establishment for posting to Cadet unit, 16 1 18.
Brooksbank, Actg. Bmdr. P.	20	11 17	To Base, sick, 6 8 18. Reposted 25 8 18. Gassed, 16 10 18.
Bropley, Gnr. R.	22	1 18	To Guards Division, 13 2 18.
Brown, Gnr. F.	8	7 17	From 371st S.B. Gassed and wounded, 14 7 17. Died, 27 7 17.
Brown, Gnr. F. C.	8	7 17	From 371st S.B. Gassed, 14 7 17. To England, 27 7 17.
Brown, Cpl. J., M.M.	15	9 17	Rhine, December, 1918.

Name and Final Rank in Battery.	Date Posted to Battery.	Remarks.
Brown, Gnr. J. J.	14 6 17	Wounded, 7 7 17. To England, 19 7 17.
Brown, Gnr. H. M.	14 6 17	Rhine, December, 1918.
Brown, Gnr. R. H.	9 7 18	Wounded, 16 9 18. To England, 19 9 18.
Brown, Gnr. W.	4 2 18	Rhine, December, 1918.
Brown, Gnr. W. J.	25 2 17	To England, sick, 26 7 17.
Buchan, Gnr. J.	20 11 17	To Base, sick, 8 7 18.
Buck, Gnr. C.	15 9 17	To England, accidentally injured, 18 11 17.
Budd, Gnr. A. E. H.	10 3 18	To Base, sick, 30 5 18.
Burtwistle, Gnr. W. (Came out with Battery.)		To Base, sick, 27 5 17.
Butterworth, Gnr. W.	25 11 16	Wounded, 7 7 17. To England, 22 7 17.
Carr, B.Q.M.S. D.	4 12 16	To 116th S.B, 10 8 17.
Carter, Gnr. H.	29 1 17	Wounded, 21 8 17. Accidentally injured and to England, 18 1 18.
Carter, Gnr. J. W.	25 2 17	Rhine, December, 1918.
Chamberlain, Actg. Bmdr. H.	8 7 17	From 371st S.B. Wounded, 11 7 17. To England, sick, 14 10 17.
Chandler, Whlr. Gnr. F. J. H.	24 10 18	Rhine, December, 1918.
Chaplain, Gnr. J.	4 12 16	Wounded, 7 7 17. To England, 11 7 17.
Chaplin, Gnr. W.	8 7 17	From 371st S.B. Gassed, 19 7 17. To England, sick, 18 8 17.
Chapman, Gnr. F. G.........		Rhine, December, 1918.
Cherry, Gnr. W. H.	8 7 17	From 371st S.B. Died from wounds, 20 7 17.
Chisholme, Gnr. J. G.	19 11 17	Wounded, 6 4 18. To England, 10 4 18.
Clapton, Cpl. A. E.	8 7 17	From 371st S.B. Gassed, 24 7 17. To England, 5 8 17.
Clarke, Gnr. A.	31 8 17	Rhine, December, 1918.
Clarke, Gnr. J.	31 8 17	To Base, sick, 4 11 17.
Clarke, Gnr. P.	11 5 18	To England, sick, 3 7 18.
Cleator, Gnr. R. B.	25 2 17	Killed in action, 11 7 17.
Clifford, Gnr. H.	4 2 18	Rhine, December, 1918.
Clough, Gnr. H.	20 11 16	To England, sick, 26 11 17.
Clubbs, Gnr. J.	19 11 17	To England, sick, 25 1 18.
Cochrane, Gnr. J. F.	25 11 16	To Base, sick, 31 7 17.
Coe, Sergt. A. W.	27 9 17	From 216th S.B. To Base, sick, 23 6 18. Reposted to Battery, 4 7 18.
Cole, Gnr. J. W.	19 11 17	Rhine, December, 1918.
Collins, Gnr. A.	2 12 16	Wounded, 5 7 17. To Base, 5 9 17.
Collins, Ftr.-S.-S. G.	12 9 17	To England, sick, 29 3 18.
Collins, Gnr. H.	27 8 18	Rhine, December, 1918.
Collyer, Gnr. H.	15 7 18	Rhine, December, 1918.
Colville, Gnr. H. V.	26 7 17	From 5th Army Pool. Wounded, 21 8 17. To Base, sick, 2 4 18.
Cooke, Gnr. H. J.	19 11 17	To Base, sick, 1 2 18.
Cooper, Gnr. E. G.	8 4 18	Rhine, December, 1918.
Cove, Gnr. W. J.	4 12 16	To England, wounded, 2 8 17.
Cowdell, Gnr. S.	8 7 17	From 371st S.B. Wounded, 24 7 17. To Base, 6 8 17.
Cross, Gnr. A. G.	8 4 18	To England, accidentally injured, 24 4 18.
Cross, Actg. Bmdr. H. (Came out with Battery.)		To Home Establishment, 23 5 17, for posting to Cadet unit.
Crossley, Gnr. J. E.	8 7 17	From 371st S.B. Gassed, 14 7 17. To Base, 23 8 17.
Crowe, Gnr. D.	31 8 17	Sick about February, 1918. To Base.
Crowe, Gnr. R. J.	8 7 17	From 371st S.B. Gassed, 14 7 17. To England, 27 7 17.
Crute, Gnr. T. R.	3 6 17	To Base, sick, 28 12 17.
Cunningham, Ftr.-S.-S. J.	9 5 18	From 248th S.B. Wounded,, 25 9 18. In hospital, 12 12 18.
Cunningham, Gnr. J.	3 6 17	Wounded, 7 7 17. To England, 19 7 17.
Daniels, Gnr. J. R.	27 8 18	Rhine, December, 1918.
Darby, Gnr. A. W. C.	8 4 18	To England, sick, 28 6 18.
Darlington, Gnr. W. J. ...	23 5 17	Wounded, 16 9 17. To England.
Darwent, Gnr. J.	20 11 16	Wounded, 7 7 17. To England, 22 7 17.
Davey, Gnr. H.	15 7 18	Gassed, 15 10 18. In hospital, 12 12 18.
Davidson, Gnr. F.	25 5 18	Rhine, December, 1918.
Davies, Gnr. A. W.	23 12 17	About January, 1918, to Base, sick.
Davies, Gnr. G. S.	15 7 18	To England, sick, 19 9 18.

Name and Final Rank in Battery.	Date Posted to Battery.	Remarks.
Davies, W. M.	10 1 18	Rhine, December, 1918.
Day, Gnr. E.	19 11 17	To England, sick, 28 12 17.
Day, Gnr. T.	19 11 17	Rhine, December, 1918.
Dean, Gnr. J. E.	23 12 17	To England, sick, 21 1 18.
Dean, Actg. Bmdr. W. E.	8 7 17	From 371st S.B. To England, sick, 28 1 18.
Dobbs, Gnr. G.	23 5 17	Wounded, 18 6 17. To Base, 30 6 17.
Dolan, Gnr. D.	23 5 17	Wounded, 7 7 17. To Base, 11 9 17.
Dollard, Sergt. P. H.	11 6 17	To 5th Army H.A., 6 7 17.
Dolphin, Gnr. A. E.	16 12 17	Rhine, December, 1918.
Dolphin, Gnr. J.	8 7 17	From 371st S.B. Gassed, 13 7 17. To England, sick, 28 1 18.
Douglas, Cpl. A. J.	4 12 16	To Base, sick, 10 8 17. Reposted to Battery, 25 8 17. To England, sick, 19 12 17.
Draper, Gnr. T.	23 12 17	Wounded, 6 4 18. To Base, 17 4 18.
Dyson, Gnr A. A.	23 5 17	Rhine, December, 1918.
Drummond, Gnr. W.	27 8 18	Rhine, December, 1918.
Dyson, Gnr. A. A.	23 5 17	Rhine, December, 1918.
Eastwood, Gnr. A.	4 2 18	Rhine, December, 1918.
Eaton, Gnr. W. G.	25 2 17	To Base, sick, 4 9 17.
Eborn, Gnr. G.	21 12 16	To Base, sick, 30 1 18.
Ellis, Gnr. A. E.	4 2 18	In hospital, sick, 12 12 18.
Evans, Bmdr. E.	15 9 17	Wounded, 30 10 18. Rhine, December, 1918.
Elsam, Gnr. E. T.	4 2 18	Rhine, December, 1918.
Fairhurst, Gnr. T.	8 7 17	From 371st S.B. Gassed, 14 7 17. To Base, sick, 11 7 18.
Ferguson, Gnr. D.	19 1 18	Rhine, December, 1918.
Ferris, Gnr. T.	19 1 18	Rhine, December, 1918.
Fielding, Gnr. G. H.	25 5 18	Accidentally injured, 22 10 18.
Fish, Gnr. J. W.	25 7 17	Wounded, 1 1 18. Died from wounds, 10 1 18.
Fleming, Actg. Bmdr. P. (Came out with Battery.)		To Base, sick, 9 6 17.
Fletcher, Gnr. W. J.	25 2 17	Rhine, December, 1918.
Foley, Gnr. A.	8 7 17	From 371st S.B. Gassed, 14 7 17. To England, 24 7 17.
Follows, Gnr. P. S.	24 1 17	Gassed, 14 7 17. To England, sick, 8 11 17.
France, Gnr. J. W.	20 11 16	Rhine, December, 1918.
Fraser, Gnr. H.	8 7 17	From 371st S.B. Gassed, 14 7 17. To England, 7 8 17.
Freeman, Gnr. W. P.	1 12 17	Rhine, December, 1918.
French, Gnr. J. G.	25 5 18	Rhine, December, 1918.
Frost, Gnr. A. J.	8 7 17	From 371st S.B. Rhine, December, 1918.
Fryer, Gnr. E. P.	25 2 17	Gassed, 14 7 17. Killed, 6 4 18.
Fryer, Gnr. W.	4 17	To Base, sick, 10 6 17.
Fuller, Gnr. G. R.	15 9 17	Rhine, December, 1918.
Gammon, Gnr. A. E. (Came out with Battery.)		To England, sick, 25 5 17.
Gelder, Gnr. E.	17 7 17	From 27th S.B. Wounded, 1 12 17. To England, 9 12 17.
Giddings, Gnr. W. T.	4 12 16	Wounded, 7 7 17. Wounded, 17 8 18. To England, 20 8 18
Gill, Gnr. W. H.	8 7 17	From 371st S.B. Gassed, 14 7 17. Died from wounds, 4 9 17.
Gilliver, Gnr. G.	4 12 16	Wounded, 7 7 17. To England, 29 7 17.
Gillott, Sergt. W. S.	5 12 16	Wounded, 18 6 17. To England, 3 7 17.
Glover, Gnr. R.	4 2 18	Accidentally injured, 6 10 18. To Base, 13 11 18.
Godfrey, Gnr. T. W.	25 11 16	To 51st H.A.G., 21 7 17.
Goldsmith, Actg. Bmdr. A. H.	27 12 16	Gassed, 14 7 17. To England, sick, 7 7 18.
Gorst, Ftr.-S.-S. J. J.	20 4 18	Wounded, 25 9 18. To England, 29 9 18.
Gowing, Gnr. J.	25 7 17	To England, sick, 21 11 17.
Graham, Gnr. M. D.	4 17	To Base, sick, 13 5 17.
Graham, Gnr. R.	11 6 17	To 5th Army H. A., 6 7 17.
Grant, Cpl. W.	30 6 18	Rhine, December, 1918.
Greaves, Gnr. G. H.	8 7 17	From 371st S.B. Gassed, 14 7 17. Wounded, 8 8 18. To England, 16 8 18.

Name and Final Rank in Battery.	Date Posted to Battery.	Remarks.
Green, Gnr. P.	25 7 17	Wounded, 16 9 17. To Base, 28 10 17.
Griffin, Gnr. J.	16 1 18	Rhine, December, 1918.
Grinter, Gnr. E. E.	4 12 16	Wounded, 11 7 17. To England, 26 7 17.
Guy, Gnr. E.	23 1 17	Gassed, 18 7 17. To England, 24 7 17.
Hall, Gnr. G.	26 7 17	From 5th Army Pool. To Base, sick, 6 1 18.
Hall, Gnr. H.	26 7 17	From 5th Army Pool. Accidentally injured, 7 8 17. To Base, 15 9 17.
Hall, Gnr. L.	28 9 18	Rhine, December, 1918.
Hall, Gnr. N.	25 11 16	To England, sick, 21 7 17.
Halliday, Gnr. W. A.	11 6 17	To 5th Army H.A., 6 7 17.
Hambrook, Gnr. H. W.	26 7 17	From 5th Army Pool. Wounded, 18 10 17. To Base, sick, 16 3 18.
Hampson, Gnr. R.	25 8 17	To England, sick, 9 2 18.
Hancock, Bmdr. J.	11 6 17	To 5th Army H.A., 6 7 17.
Hancocks, Bmdr. F. A.	8 7 17	From 371st S.B. Wounded, 11 7 17.
Hanslow, Gnr. J.	25 11 16	Rhine, December, 1918.
Hanson, Gnr. W.	21 10 18	Rhine, December, 1918.
Harding, Gnr. C.	25 8 17	To England, sick, 20 12 17.
Harding, Gnr. S. C.	11 6 17	To 5th Army Pool, 6 7 17.
Hardy, Gnr. T.	25 5 18	Rhine, December, 1918.
Harrington, Gnr. A.	25 11 16	Rhine, December, 1918.
Harris, B.S.M. G.	3 5 18	Rhine, December, 1918.
Harris, Gnr. J. W.	8 7 17	From 371st S.B. Gassed, 14 7 17. Wounded, 21 8 17. To Base, sick, 2 10 18.
Harrison, Gnr. T. W.	26 7 17	From 5th Army Pool. To England, sick, 7 11 17.
Hassall, Gnr. T. H.	3 8 17	To England, sick, 28 5 18.
Hatton, Gnr. J.	13 3 17	Rhine, December, 1918.
Hawkey, Gnr. W. E.	2 12 16	To Base, sick, 31 8 17.
Hawkins, Gnr. G. A.	16 1 18	Rhine, December, 1918.
Hawtin, Gnr. C. H.	25 8 17	Rhine, December, 1918.
Hazell, Gnr. E.	8 7 17	From 371st S.B. Gassed, 14 7 17.
Heeley, Gnr. L.	15 7 18	Rhine, December, 1918.
Hesketh, Gnr. W.	13 2 18	Rhine, December, 1918.
Herbert, Gnr. G.	26 7 17	From 5th Army Pool. To Base, sick, 24 11 17.
Hewson, Gnr. S.	4 2 18	Rhine, December, 1918.
Hicklin, Gnr. A. W.	31 8 17	To England, sick, 24 12 17.
Hill, Gnr. G.	21 10 18	Rhine, December, 1918.
Hill, Gnr. H. H.	27 12 16	Killed in action, 12 7 17.
Hill, Gnr. T. G.	21 9 17	To England, sick, 3 12 17.
Hillier, Gnr. R.	25 5 18	Rhine, December, 1918.
Hilling, Gnr. A. W.	25 9 18	Rhine, December, 1918.
Hills, Gnr. F.	25 8 17	To England, sick, 18 9 17.
Hinds, Gnr. S.	8 7 17	From 371st S.B. To England, gassed, 6 8 17.
Hitchin, Gnr. F.	25 11 16	Wounded, 18 6 17. To England, 23 6 17.
Hoar, Bmdr. R.	5 12 16	To England, sick, 10 8 17.
Hodgkinson, Gnr. J.	25 11 16	Wounded, 23 6 17. To England, 28 6 17.
Hole, Gnr. J. H.	8 7 17	From 371st S.B. Rhine, Dec., 1918.
Hollingworth, Gnr. W. L.	25 11 16	Died from wounds, 27 7 17.
Holmes, Gnr. A.	11 6 17	To Base, sick, about July, 1917.
Holmes, Gnr. G. W.	25 2 17	Wounded, 7 7 17. To England, 13 7 17.
Holmes, Gnr. T.	25 8 17	To England, sick, 23 9 17.
Hood, Gnr. A.	26 7 17	From 5th Army Pool. Wounded, 30 10 18.
Hopgood, Gnr. W.	8 8 18	Rhine, December, 1918.
Hanby, Gnr. W. S.	25 11 16	Wounded, 22 6 17. To England, 25 6 17.
Horton, Gnr. J. A.	11 6 17	To 5th Army H.A., 6 7 17.
Howard, Gnr. A.	19 1 18	To Base, sick, 28 2 18.
Howard, Gnr. W.	19 11 18	Rhine, December, 1918.
Hughes, Gnr. A.	26 7 17	To England, sick, 15 4 18.
Hughes, Gnr. W.	26 7 17	From 5th Army Pool. Wounded, 3 8 17. To Base, 6 11 17.
Hulse, Bmdr. W.	25 8 17	Accidentally injured, 5 2 18. To Base, 4 4 18. Reposted to battery, 24 4 18. Rhine, December, 1918.

Name and Final Rank in Battery.	Date Posted to Battery.	Remarks.
Humphrey, Gnr. W.	25 8 17	To England, sick, 4 2 18.
Humphreys, Gnr. W. J. ...	11 6 17	To 5th Army H.A., about 6 7 17
Hunt, Gnr. A. J. ..../...	25 5 18	Rhine, December, 1918.
Hunt, Ftr.-Gnr. E.	29 11 17	Rhine, December, 1918.
Hunter, Gnr. A.	28 9 18	Rhine, December, 1918.
Hutchings, Gnr. W. J.	31 8 17	Rhine, December, 1918.
Huxley, Gnr. H. W.	26 7 17	From 5th Army Pool. To Base, 3 9 17.
Ingham, Gnr. R.	20 11 16	Wounded, 1 12 17. To England, 18 12 17.
Ingram, Gnr. G. H.	21 9 17	Rhine, December, 1918.
Isherwood, Bmdr. W.	(Came out with Battery.)	To Base, sick, 30 5 17.
Jackson, Gnr. B.	25 8 17	Rhine, December, 1918.
Jacobs, Gnr. M.	28 9 18	Rhine, December, 1918.
James, Gnr. J. C.	25 8 17	To Base, 31 10 17.
Jarvis, Gnr. H. H.	26 7 17	To England, sick, 28 3 18.
Jenkins, Gnr. S.	8 7 17	From 371st S.B. Gassed, 14 7 17.
Jenkins, Gnr. W. H.	8 11 17	Rhine, December, 1918.
Jennes, Gnr. W.	4 12 16	To England, sick, 23 3 18.
Jennings, Gnr H...............	25 8 17	To England, sick, 27 1 18.
Johnson, Gnr. C.	28 9 18	To England, sick, 4 10 18.
Johnson, Gnr. C. L.	26 7 17	Wounded, 24 8 18. To England, 14 9 18.
Johnson, Gnr. F. G.	28 9 18	Rhine, December, 1918.
Johnson, Gnr. G.	25 8 17	Rhine, December, 1918.
Jones, Gnr. D.	(Came out with Battery.)	To Base, sick, 11 6 17.
Jones, Gnr. E. J.	25 8 17	To Base, sick, 20 4 18.
Jones, Gnr. G.	25 8 17	To England, sick, 22 11 17.
Jones, Gnr. H.	26 8 17	From 60th S.B., to 81st S.B., 6 4 18
Jones, Bmdr. J. E.	25 9 16	Rhine, December, 1918.
Jones, Gnr. L. C.	(Came out with Battery.)	To England, sick, 18 5 17.
Jones, Gnr. R.	25 2 17	Rhine, December, 1918
Jones, Gnr. T. H.	2 6 17	Rhine, December, 1918.
Joynson, Gnr. A.	16 9 17	Wounded, 13 12 17. To England, 17 12 17.
Jukes, Cpl. H.	5 12 16	Killed in action, 7 7 17.
Keddie, Gnr. F.	23 1 18	Rhine, December, 1918.
Keeble, Gnr. C. E.	25 11 16	To England, sick, 5 9 17.
Kerr, Gnr. J.	25 2 17	Wounded, 7 7 17. To England, 16 7 17.
Kingdon, Gnr. H. H.	25 8 17	Rhine, December, 1918.
Kirby, Gnr. E.	24 5 18	Rhine, December, 1918.
Knight, Gnr. E. T.	25 8 17	To England, sick, 19 12 17.
Knight, Gnr. H.	25 8 17	Rhine, December, 1918.
Knight, Gnr. J. W.	25 8 17	To Base, sick, 25 1 18.
Knightson, Gnr. H.	(About Jan., 1918.)	To Base, sick, 12 8 18.
Lamb, Gnr. R.	25 8 17	To England, sick, 19 10 17.
Lamb, Gnr. W. J.	25 8 17	To England, sick, 7 3 18.
Lambert, Gnr. J.	25 7 17	Wounded, 1 8 17. To England, 7 8 17.
Lambeth, Gnr. A.	19 11 18	From 326th S.B. Rhine, December, 1918.
Large, Gnr. C. H.	1 3 18	To England, sick, 21 6 18.
Latimer, Act. Bmdr. T. L., M.M.	25 8 17	To England, sick, 25 9 18.
Lawrence, Gnr. W. H.	2 12 16	Died from wounds, 3 7 17.
Lawson, Gnr. J. W.	28 9 18	To Base, sick, about January, 1918.
Leatt, Gnr. B.	28 9 18	Rhine, December, 1918.
Lee, Gnr. T.	19 1 18	Rhine, December, 1918.
Le Fevre, Gnr. W. J.	1 3 18	Rhine, December, 1918.
Legge, Sergt. E. H.	6 12 16	Wounded, 24 7 17. To England, 17 8 17.
Lewis, Gnr. E.	8 7 17	From 371st S.B. Gassed, 14 7 17.
Linsell, Gnr. G. W.	31 12 17	To England, 6 3 18, sick.
Linton, Cpl. E. B.	8 7 17	From 371st S.B. Gassed, 14 7 17. To Base, sick, 9 3 18. Reposted from Base, 24 4 18. Wounded, 4 6 18. Rhine, December, 1918.
Lloyd, Gnr. J.	25 8 17	To Base, sick, December, 1917.
Lomas, Gnr. T.	(Came out with Battery.)	To Base, sick, 27 7 17.
Lucas, Gnr. F.	9 7 18	Rhine, December, 1918.
Lumb, Gnr. G.	1 3 18	To Base, sick, 11 10 18.

Name and Final Rank in Battery.	Date Posted to Battery.		Remarks.
Lumsden, Gnr. S.	9	7 18	Rhine, December, 1918.
Lyle, Gnr. H. S.	25	8 17	Rhine, December, 1918.
Macintosh, Gnr. W.	25	2 17	Rhine, December, 1918.
Mackie, Sergt. W. G.	4	12 16	Rhine, December, 1918.
March, Gnr. W. T.	3	8 17	To England, sick, 15 10 17.
Marrow, Gnr. J. B.	8	7 17	From 371st S.B. Gassed, 14 7 17. To Base, 12 8 17.
Marsden, Gnr. W. H.	10	1 18	Rhine, December, 1918.
Martin, Gnr. G. A.	25	8 17	Rhine, December, 1918.
Maslin, Gnr. F. E.	10	1 18	To England, sick, 8 3 18.
Mason, Gnr. T.	8	7 17	From 371st S.B. Gassed, 14 7 17. Accidentally injured, 7 8 17. To Base, 18 9 17.
Matheson, Gnr. D. G.	8	7 17	From 371st S.B. Gassed, 14 7 17. To England, 3 8 17.
Matheson, Gnr. E.	13	3 17	Wounded, 1 5 17. Killed in action, 30 12 17.
Maughan, Gnr. W. H.	25	8 17	To Base, sick, 21 9 18.
Mayes, Gnr. A.	10	1 18	To England, sick, 6 2 18.
Maynes, Gnr. W.	19	1 18	To Base, sick, about February, 1918.
McCusker, Gnr. B.	14	1 18	Rhine, December, 1918.
McDowall, Gnr. J.	25	2 17	Wounded, 7 7 17. To England, 10 7 17.
McFarlane, J.	25	2 17	Killed in action, 11 7 17.
McGill, Bmdr. D.	25	2 17	Gassed, 14 7 17. Wounded, 2 3 18. To England, 8 3 18.
McGuinness, Gnr. J. M. K.	10	1 18	Rhine, December, 1918.
McInnes, Gnr. D.	5	12 17	To England, sick, 3 2 18.
McKevitt, Gnr. B.	4	12 16	To England, sick, 8 9 17.
McKinney, Bmdr. P.	31	8 17	Rhine, December, 1918.
McLaren, Gnr. S.	8	7 17	From 371st S.B. Gassed, 14 7 17. Died, 20 7 17.
McLean, Gnr. C.	31	8 17	Rhine, December, 1918.
McManus, Gnr. F.	4	12 16	Wounded, 26 11 17. Rhine, December, 1918.
McRae, Gnr. A.	13	1 18	Wounded, 2 2 18. To Base, sick, 5 10 18.
Meadows, Sergt. F. C. (Came out with Battery.)			Accidentally injured, 16 5 17. To England, 19 5 17.
Melsom, Actg. Bmdr. E. H.	27	12 16	To Base, 8 8 17. Reposted from Base, 8 11 17. To England, sick, 28 1 18.
Merrill, Gnr. W.	10	1 18	To Base, sick, 20 7 18.
Moor, Sergt. S. F.	2	12 16	Rhine, December, 1918.
Moore, Gnr. J.	2	12 16	Wounded, 7 7 17. To England, 13 7 17.
Moore, Gnr. W. E.	24	5 18	Rhine, December, 1918.
Morgan, Gnr. E. A.	14	1 18	To Base, sick, 14 9 18.
Morley, Gnr. C. E.	15	9 17	Wounded, 5 12 17.
Morris, Gnr. J. L.	25	2 17	To Base, sick, 8 9 17.
Mottershead, Actg. Bmdr. F.	25	2 17	Rhine, December, 1918.
Miller, Gnr. D. W.	31	8 17	To Base, sick, 23 5 18.
Miller, Gnr. H.	31	8 17	To England, accidentally injured, 11 4 18.
Miller, Bmdr. S. N.	25	2 17	Gassed, 14 7 17. Rhine, Dec., 1918.
Millward, Gnr. W.	8	7 17	From 371st S.B. Gassed, 14 7 17. To England, for munition work, 24 8 17.
Miskin, Gnr. J. B. D.	27	12 16	Transferred to Royal Engineers, 22 10 17.
Mitchell, Gnr. H.	31	8 17	Wounded, 15 12 17. To England, 17 12 17.
Munday, Actg. Bmdr. A. ...	10	1 18	Rhine, December, 1918.
Munro, B.Q.M.S. L. W. ...	14	9 17	From 27th S.B. Rhine, December, 1918.
Naylor, Cpl. E.	25	11 16	Accidentally injured. To Base. Reposted to Battery, 23 3 18. Rhine, December, 1918.
Neale, Gnr. A.	31	8 17	Rhine, December, 1918.
Nethercott, Actg. Bmdr. E. W.	15	9 17	Rhine, December, 1918.
Nevin, Gnr. E.	25	12 17	From 326th S.B. To H.Q. 5th Corps H.A., 24 4 18.
Newham, Cpl. E.	25	2 17	Wounded, 7 7 17. Rhine, December, 1918.
Nicholls, Sergt. S. T., M.M.	8	7 17	From 371st S.B. Gassed, 14 7 17. Rhine, December, 1918.

Name and Final Rank in Battery.	Date Posted to Battery.	Remarks.
Nimmo, Actg. Bmdr. A. S.	5 11 16	Wounded, 26 7 17. To Base, 13 8 17.
Nixon, Whlr. Gnr. W. L.	28 12 16	Wounded, 24 3 18. To Base, 12 5 18.
Norman, Gnr. H. A.	24 1 17	Wounded, 1 12 17. To England, 6 12 17.
Northover, Gnr. H.	25 2 17	Wounded, 7 8 17. To England, 17 8 17.
Nudds, Actg. Bmdr. E.	7 12 16	Wounded and Gassed, 22 7 17. To England, 28 7 17.
O'Connor, Gnr. D.	10 1 18	To Base, sick, 28 2 18.
Onley, Gnr. T.	25 7 17	To Base, sick, about January, 1918.
O'Rourke, Gnr. L.	21 9 17	Rhine, December, 1918.
Oswald, Gnr. A.	8 7 17	From 371st S.B. Died from wounds, 11 7 17.
O'Toole, Gnr. T.	4 9 18	Rhine, December, 1918.
Overend, Gnr. T. E.	31 8 17	Rhine, December, 1918.
Overett, Gnr. F.	24 5 18	To Base, sick, 11 8 18.
Owens, Gnr. P.	25 7 17	To England, sick, 22 9 17.
Parnell, Sergt. E., M.M.	1 1 17	Rhine, December, 1918.
Payne, Gnr. P.	25 2 17	Rhine, December, 1918.
Penfold, Gnr. H.	24 5 18	Rhine, December, 1918.
Peplow, Gnr. G. A.	15 11 18	Rhine, December, 1918.
Pickett, Gnr. W.	8 7 17	From 371st S.B. Killed, 14 7 17.
Pickles, Gnr. J.	8 7 17	From 371st S.B. Gassed, 14 7 17. In hospital, 12 12 18.
Pitcher, Ftr.-S.-S. A. W.	30 4 18	To 121st H.B., 26 7 18.
Pitkeathley, Gnr. H. C.	24 5 18	Rhine, December, 1918.
Pole, Gnr. J.	8 7 17	From 371st S.B. Wounded, 26 9 18. To England, 29 9 18.
Pomfret, Gnr. L.	25 7 17	To England, sick, 11 1 18.
Pope, Gnr. E.	13 8 17	From No. 1 Reinforcement Company. To England, sick, 31 1 18.
Potter, Cpl. T.	25 2 17	Wounded, 20 6 17. To England, sick, 29 1 18.
Potts, Gnr. H. H.	13 11 18	Rhine, December, 1918.
Preece, Gnr. A.	15 11 18	Rhine, December, 1918.
Pressland, Gnr. J.	15 11 18	Rhine, December, 1918.
Price, Cpl. F.	4 12 16	To Base, sick, 1 3 18. Reposted to Battery, 2 5 18. Rhine, December, 1918.
Price, Gnr. T.	25 2 17	Gassed, 18 7 17. To Base.
Purdy, Gnr. A.	25 7 17	Gassed, 1 1 18. To England, 7 1 18.
Putt, Sergt. B.	25 11 16	To England, sick, 4 9 17.
Race, Gnr. T. H.	17 12 17	Rhine, December, 1918.
Ransley, Gnr. F.	15 11 18	Rhine, December, 1918.
Redrup, Sergt. C.	27 9 17	From 216th S.B. To England, sick, 5 1 19.
Reeve, Gnr. J.	15 11 18	Rhine, December, 1918.
Reid, Gnr. J.	26 2 17	To Base, sick, 24 8 17.
Richards, Gnr. A.	17 12 17	To England, sick, 8 3 18.
Riley, Gnr. F.	19 1 18	Rhine, December, 1918.
Robertson, Actg . Bmdr. R. C.	25 8 17	Wounded, 27 5 18. To England, 31 5 18.
Robinson, Gnr. J. H.	18 11 16	Gassed, 14 7 17. To England, 2 8 17.
Rochford, Gnr. P.	15 11 18	Rhine, December, 1918.
Rogerson, Gnr. J.	15 11 18	Rhine, December, 1918.
Ruff, Gnr. T.	8 7 17	From 371st S.B. Wounded, 4 5 18. Rhine, December, 1918.
Sankey, Ftr.-Gnr. S.	5 2 18	Rhine, December, 1918.
Saulter, Gnr. E.	22 1 18	To England, sick, 3 7 18.
Scaife, Gnr. C. G.	8 7 17	From 371st S.B. Gassed, 14 7 17. To England, 30 7 17.
Scutt, Gnr. E.	15 9 17	To England, sick, 24 11 17.
Seaman, Gnr. W. D.	22 1 18	Rhine, December, 1918.
Shaddick, Smith-Gnr. F. V.	16 6 17	Gassed, 17 7 17. To Base, 14 9 17.
Sharp, Cpl. F.	27 12 16	Accidentally killed, 24 11 17.
Sharp, Gnr. H.	(Came out with Battery.)	Died from wounds, 2 7 17.
Shearing, Gnr. S. F.	27 12 16	Gassed, 14 7 17. To England, 6 8 17.
Sherman, Gnr. D. J.	21 9 17	Rhine, December, 1918.
Siedenberg, Cpl. E.	6 12 16	To Base, sick, 17 12 17.
Sinclair, Gnr. A.	13 3 17	To England, sick, 11 1 18.
Slade, Gnr. H.	14 7 17	To Base, sick, 28 10 17.
Slaney, Gnr. G. H.	15 9 17	Wounded 30 10 18. To England, 2 11 18.
Slaughter, Gnr. A.	3 8 17	Rhine, December, 1918.

Name and Final Rank in Battery.	Date Posted to Battery.	Remarks.
Small, Gnr. J.	14 7 17	Wounded, 7 8 17. To England, 12 8 17.
Smart, Gnr. A.	25 8 17	Wounded, 16 9 17. To Base, 26 9 17.
Smith, Actg. Bmdr. J.	8 7 17	From 371st S.B. Gassed, 14 7 17.
Smith, Ftr.-Cpl. L.	11 12 17	Taken on strength of R.G.A. Clearing House, Dover, 15 2 18.
Smith, Gnr. R. F.	21 9 17	Accidentally injured, 3 2 18. To Base, 16 3 18.
Smith, Actg.-Bmdr. W. J.	8 5 18	To 242nd S.B., 8 10 18.
Smithson, Gnr. J.	(Came out with Battery.)	To Base, sick, 10 6 17.
Snook, Gnr. T. V.	14 7 17	To Base, sick, 12 7 18.
Southcott, Gnr. E. G.	14 7 17	To Base sick, 23 12 17.
Spratley, Gnr. F. W.	24 6 18	Rhine, December, 1918.
Squires, Bmdr. J.	18 4 17	From V 36 T.M. Battery. To 255 S.B., 13 6 17.
Stace, Sergt. H. J. B.	8 7 17	From 371st S.B. Gassed, 14 7 17. To England, 11 8 17.
Stanford, Gnr. W.	21 9 17	Rhine, December, 1918.
Stead, Sergt. C., M.M.	8 7 17	From 371st S.B. Wounded, 24 7 17. Rhine, December, 1918.
Steel, Gnr. J.	14 7 17	Wounded, 27 7 17. To England, 1 8 17.
Steel, B.S.M. J. J.	14 2 17	Killed, 25 1 18.
Stephenson, Gnr. F.	14 7 17	Wounded, 27 11 17. To Base.
Stewart, Gnr. G.	(Came out with Battery.)	Killed, 1 5 17.
Stewart, Cpl. H.	4 12 16	Wounded, 5 7 17. To England, 17 7 17.
Stott, Gnr. G. P.	13 3 17	Rhine, December, 1918.
Straw, Gnr. W.	15 11 18	Rhine, December, 1918.
Stringer, Whlr.-Sergt. T. B.	11 5 18	Wounded, 17 9 18. Wounded, 26 9 18. To England, 29 9 18.
Stroud, Gnr. F. G.	19 1 18	Rhine, December, 1918.
Sweetingham, Actg. Bmdr. J., M.M.	27 12 16	Wounded, 6 12 17. To England, 15 12 17.
Taffs, Actg. Bmdr. P. A.	2 10 17	Rhine, December, 1918.
Tanner, Sergt. F. A.	6 12 16	Rhine, December, 1918.
Tavender, Gnr. T. C.	9 7 18	Wounded, 13 9 18. Rhine, December, 1918.
Taylor, Actg. Bmdr. B. F.	25 8 17	Wounded, 12 4 18. To England, sick, 4 10 18.
Taylor, Bmdr. J. T.	3 8 17	Rhine, December, 1918.
Tee, Gnr. A. E.	25 7 17	To England, sick, 15 11 17.
Thain, Gnr. A.	3 8 17	To England, sick, 28 11 17.
Thomas, Gnr. J.	15 9 17	Rhine, December, 1918.
Thompson, Gnr. J. L.	4 12 16	Shell shock, 5 7 17. To England 27 8 17.
Thomson, Gnr. V. E.	22 1 18	To Base, sick, 30 5 18.
Tickner, Gnr. P.	3 8 17	Wounded, 21 8 17. Wounded, 7 1 18. To England 1 3 18.
Tissington, Gnr. W. H.	8 7 17	From 371st S.B. Gassed, 14 7 17. To England, 8 8 17.
Tomlinson, Gnr. J. H. G.	2 10 17	Rhine, December, 1918.
Tomlinson, Gnr. H. W.	3 8 17	To Base, sick, 12 3 18.
Toone, Gnr. C.	21 12 16	Wounded, 23 6 17. To England, 1 7 17.
Torrance, Gnr. A.	25 2 17	Wounded, 7 7 17. To England, 14 7 17.
Tromans, Gnr. T.	25 11 16	Wounded, 7 8 17. To England, 16 9 18, sick.
Trotter, Bmdr. B.	3 8 17	Rhine, December, 1918.
Tunnicliffe, Gnr. S.	3 8 17	Wounded, 7 8 17. To England, 20 8 17.
Turnbull, Actg. Bmdr. R. S.	3 8 17	Rhine, December, 1918.
Turner, Cpl. A. V.	4 3 18	From 336th S.B. Rhine, December, 1918.
Turner, Gnr. J.	2 10 17	To England, sick, 6 1 18.
Turner, Gnr. R.	12 9 18	Rhine, December, 1918.
Turner, Sergt. W., M.M.	5 12 16	Wounded, 25 9 18. To England, 1 10 18.
Turner, Gnr. W. A.	3 8 17	Rhine, December, 1918.
Turnock, Gnr. W.	25 8 17	Rhine, December, 1918.
Turvey, Gnr. C. H.	15 7 18	To England, sick, 18 11 18.
Tyler, Gnr. F. R.	25 8 17	Rhine, December, 1918.
Upton, Gnr. H. G.	21 9 17	Rhine, December, 1918.
Vaux, Gnr. R.	25 11 16	Accidentally injured, 7 10 18.
Veitch, Actg. Bmdr. J. R.	2 10 17	Rhine, December, 1918.

Name and Final Rank in Battery.	Date Posted to Battery.	Remarks.
Venns, Gnr. G.	1 7 17	Wounded, 7 5 18. To Base, 16 5 18.
Ventom, Gnr. G. W.	15 7 18	Rhine, December, 1918.
Viney, Gnr. G. T.	1 7 17	Wounded, 22 7 17. Gassed, 27 7 17. To Base, sick, 24 8 17.
Waite, Gnr. E. M.	5 2 18	Rhine, December, 1918.
Wakeham, Gnr. A.	3 8 17	Wounded, 1 12 17. To England, 7 12 17.
Ward, Gnr. F. H.	5 2 18	To Base, sick, 3 9 18.
Waring, Gnr. C.	11 9 18	Rhine, December, 1918.
Warne, Gnr. J.	31 8 17	Rhine, December, 1918.
Warner, Gnr. A.	24 1 17	Wounded, 30 12 17. To Base.
Watson, Gnr. J.	5 2 18	Rhine, December, 1918.
Watts, Gnr. J.	8 7 17	From 371st S.B. Gassed, 14 7 17. To England, 22 7 17.
Watts, Gnr. T. G.	5 2 18	Rhine, December, 1918.
Wearmouth, Gnr. R. W. ...	5 2 18	Rhine, December, 1918.
Webb, Gnr. A.	3 8 17	Wounded, 22 8 17. To Base, 28 10 17.
Welton, Gnr. E.	3 8 17	Wounded, 21 8 17. To England, sick, 8 1 17.
Wharf, Actg. Bmdr. J. R.	3 8 17	To England, sick, 8 1 18.
Wheatley, Gnr. J.	15 7 18	In hospital, 12 12 18.
White, Gnr. W. .... about	17 9 18	Killed in action, 24 9 18.
Whitehouse, Gnr. J.	8 7 17	From 371st S.B. Gassed, 14 7 17. Killed in action, 26 12 17.
Wickenden, Gnr. J.	3 6 17	To England, sick, 15 6 17.
Wilcock, Gnr. W.	16 12 17	To Base, sick, January, 1918.
Wild, Gnr. J. W.	8 5 18	Rhine, December, 1918.
Wilkinson, Gnr. J. G.	8 7 17	From 371st S.B. Wounded, 14 7 17. Died from wounds, 20 7 17.
Wilkinson, Gnr. S. F.	16 12 17	To Base, January, 1918.
Williams, Gnr. A.	8 5 18	Rhine, December, 1918.
Williams, Gnr. G.	5 2 18	Left Battery, 1 2 18, sick.
Williams, Gnr. H. F.	5 2 18	In hospital, 12 12 18.
Williams, Gnr. T. R.	31 8 17	To England, sick, 3 1 18.
Williamson, Bmdr. H.	8 7 17	From 371st S.B. Gassed, 13 7 17. To England, 2 8 17.
Williamson, Gnr. W. J. ...	8 5 18	Wounded, 30 10 18. To England, 4 11 18.
Willmott, Gnr. H. W.	5 2 18	Accidentally injured, 25 5 18. To Base, sick, 7 8 18.
Wilson, Gnr. C. ....., ...	5 2 18	Rhine, December, 1918.
Wilson, Gnr. J. W.	3 8 17	Rhine, December, 1918.
Wilson, Gnr. T. H.	31 8 17	Wounded, 12 9 18. To England, 16 9 18.
Wingham, Gnr. F.	21 9 17	Accidentally injured, 5 2 18. To Base, 5 4 18.
Wood, Gnr. E.	5 2 18	Rhine, December, 1918.
Wood, Gnr. T.	4 12 16	Gassed, 14 7 17.
Woodman, Gnr. A. J.	5 2 16	Rhine, December, 1918.
Workman, Gnr. W. J.	25 2 17	Taken on strength of R.G.A. Clearing Office, Dover, 15 2 18.
Worthington, Sergt. G. F.	28 1 18	To England, sick, 10 7 18.
Wren, Gnr. A. W.	5 2 18	To England, sick, 16 7 18.
Wright, Gnr. A.	7 1 17	Wounded, 7 7 17. To England, 18 7 17.
Wright, Gnr. F. W.	19 1 18	Rhine, December, 1918.
Young, Gnr. J.	4 12 16	Wounded, 7 7 17. To Base, 3 8 17.
Younger, Gnr. E.	19 1 18	To Base, sick, 23 3 18.

Summary of Casualties.

	Officers.	Other Ranks.	Total.
Killed	3	12	15
Died from wounds		12	12
Wounded	6	99	105
Gassed	3	66	69
Accidentally killed		1	1
Accidentally injured	2	16	18
Shell shock		1	1
Gassed and wounded		1	1
Total ...	14	208	222

www.ingramcontent.com/pod-product-compliance
Lightning Source LLC
Chambersburg PA
CBHW070943150426
42812CB00066B/3252/J